Iris Seed Pods ... |
Ivy *(Hedera* ... |

Japanese Iris *(Iris)* **H**
Japonica *(Spiraea japonica)* **S** *L*
Joe-Pye Weed
   (Eupatorium purpureum) **H**
Jonquil *(Narcissus)* **S** *R*

Lady's Finger *(Polygonum orientale)* **H**
Lady's Thumb
   (Polygonum Persicaria) **H**
Lantana *(Lantana)* **S** *R*
Larkspur *(Delphinium)* **S** *L*
Lavender *(Lavendula)* **H**
Liatris *(Liatris spicata)* **H**
Lichen *(Lichen)* **H**
Lilac *(Oleaceae)* **S** *L*
Lily, Easter *(Lilium)* **S** *R*
Lily, Lemon *(Lilium)* **S** *R*
Locust, Honey *(Gleditsia)* **H**
Lotus Pods *(Nelumbium Nelumbo)* **H**
Love-in-a-Mist *(Nigella damascena)* **S** *Z*
Love-in-a-Mist Pods
   (Nigella damascena) **H**
Lupine *(Lupinus)* **S** *L*

Magnolia Cones, Southern
   (Magnolia grandiflora) **H**
Magnolia Foliage, Southern
   (Magnolia grandiflora) **G** or **H**
Marigold *(Tagetes)* **S** *Z*
Milkweed Pods, Common
   (Asclepias) **H**
Millet *(Setaria italica)* **H**
Mullien *(Verbascum Thapsus)* **H**
Mimosa Pods *(Mimosa)* **H**

Nandina Berries *(Nandina domestica)* **H**
Nandina Foliage *(Nandina domestica)* **P**
Narcissus *(Narcissus)* **S** *Z*

Oak Foliage *(Quercus)* **P** or **G**
Oats *(Avena sativa)* **H**
Okra Pods *(Hibiscus esculentus)* **H**
Onion Bloom *(Allium)* **H**
Orchard Grass *(Dactylis glomerata)* **H**

Palm *(Palm)* **H**
Pansy *(Viola)* **S** *Z*
Pearly Everlasting *(Anaphalis)* **H**
Pennyroyal *(Hedeoma pulegiodes)* **H**
Peony *(Paeonia)* **S** *Z*
Pepper Pods *(Capsicum)* **H**
Periwinkle *(Vinca minor)* **G**

... *terospora andromodea)* **H**
... *(Punica Granatum)* **H**
Poppy Pods, Annual *(Papaver)* **H**
Poppy Pods, Oriental *(Papaver)* **H**
Princess Feather. See Lady's Finger
Pussywillow *(Salix)* **H**
Pyracantha *(Pyracantha)* **H**

Queen Anne's Lace *(Daucus)* **S** *Z*

Rabbit Tobacco. See Pearly Everlasting
Redbud *(Cercis)* **H**
Rhododendron *(Rhododendron)* **G**
Rose *(Rosa)* **S** *R*
Rose Foliage *(Rosa)* **P**
Rose of Sharon *(Hibiscus syriacus)* **S** *R*
Rose of Sharon Calyx
   (Hibiscus syriacus) **H**

Sage *(Salvia)* **H**
Scotch Broom *(Cytisus scoparius)* **P**
Sea Oats *(Uniola latifolia)* **H**
Snapdragon *(Antirrhinum majus)* **S** *L*
Snowball Tree *(Viburnum)* **H**
Solomon's Seal Berries, False
   (Vagnera racemosa) **H**
Sour-Wood *(Oxydendrum arboreum)* **G**
Statice *(Limonium)* **H**
Strawberry Popcorn
   (Zea Mays variety everta) **H**
Strawflower *(Helichrysum)* **H**
Sumac Seed Pod *(Rhus)* **H**
Sunflower *(Helianthus)* **S** *Z*

Tansy *(Tanacetum vulgare)* **H**
Teasel Pods *(Dipsacus)* **H**
Thyme *(Thymus vulgaris)* **H**
Tithonia or Mexican Sunflower
   (Helianthus) **S** *Z*
Tithonia Pods *(Helianthus)* **H**
Tulip *(Tulipa)* **S** *R*
Tumble Weed
   (Amaranthus graecizans) **H**

Wheat *(Triticum aestivum)* **H**
Wisteria *(Wisteria)* **H**
Wormwood, Silver King *(Artemisia)* **H**

Xeranthemum *(Xeranthemum)* **H**

Yarrow, Golden Plate *(Achillea)* **H**
Yucca *(Yucca glauca)* **H**

Zinnia *(Zinnia linearis)* **S** *Z*
Zinnia, Carpet or Lilliput *(Zinnia)* **S** *Z*
Zinnia, Common *(Zinnia)* **S** *Z*

The Dried-Flower Book

Glowing color and perfect form are possible when drying flowers by the methods described in the text. Here, an antique footed bowl of custard glass holds a mass arrangement of roses, larkspur, statice, poppy pods, strawflowers, xeranthemum, cockscomb, hydrangea, delphinium, and starflowers.

The Dried-Flower Book

A GUIDE TO METHODS AND ARRANGEMENTS

NITA COX CARICO
JANE CALVERT GUYNN

All Flower Arrangements and All Sketches by
NITA COX CARICO

1962
Doubleday & Company, Inc.
Garden City, New York

To our fathers

WILLIAM EDWIN COX

and

HENLEY ANDERSON CALVERT

in loving memory

Acknowledgments

We are deeply grateful to the people who have been directly or indirectly responsible for helping us to make this book possible:

Photographs by the Dixie Wingold Studio, of Galax, Virginia.

Mrs. Etoile Berry, sister of Nita Cox Carico, who has always been a help and inspiration to the authors.

H. N. Metcalf, Chairman of Horticulture of the Montana Federation of Garden Clubs for location and identification of western plants.

Contents

List of Illustrations

PHOTOGRAPHS

SKETCHES

Part One

DRYING
PLANT MATERIAL

I

Introduction

For many years, American women have picked the choicest flowers from their gardens, drying and arranging them to beautify their homes. Can you think of a more delightful pastime? Everyone loves to live with flowers. Think what fun it is to enjoy, out of season, the bouquets you gathered months ago.

The tradition of flower-drying was a part of the gracious living in Colonial times. This becomes apparent on a visit to Monticello, Mount Vernon, or Restored Colonial Williamsburg. The creative skill of the eighteenth-century housewife is revealed in the elaborate period designs on display here. Of course, today the techniques of flower-drying have been advanced to the point where any woman can arrange them in a style to please herself—either early period pieces or contemporary arrangements.

Drying flowers and arranging them for your home will give you pleasure and will appeal to all who see them. When your daughter receives her first corsage, you can dry these precious blooms and arrange them in a jewel box. Flowers that hold special memories for you can be dried and kept for months, even years, in a shadow box, or pressed and made into a floral picture which will last indefinitely under glass.

In reality, there is an infinite variety of decorations that you can provide for your home and at the same time derive a world of creative satisfaction in working with flowers.

Perhaps at some time you may be responsible for an altar arrangement in your church. You know what a chore and expense it often becomes to find plant material that is suitable, especially in the winter months. If you have a beautifully dried arrangement which could be kept at the church for such occasions, all the worshipers would be most grateful. In Chapter VII you will find complete instructions for making three church designs: one in white for a Christmas service; one using processed autumn leaves, goldenrod, fresh mums, and small red apples for Thanksgiving; and a pair of colorful dried arrangements to be used for the altar or elsewhere in the church at any time.

How good it makes you feel to be able to assemble a dainty compote of roses and larkspur to take to a friend who is ill—flowers that will speak of your kindness for months. Or during the cold season you can combine leaves from your collection of processed foliage with a few fresh flowers, fruits, or vegetables to make an eye-catching display.

FLOWER-DRYING A MONEY-MAKING PROPOSITION

As a lucrative avocation, flower-drying has many possibilities. Many people are interested in buying, not only individual stalks of dried plant material, but also complete arrangements including the container. A number of the photographs of arrangements, novelties, plaques, and floral pictures in this book have been taken just before placing the subject in a box to be sent to purchasers all over the country. Please see Chapter IX for instructions for transporting arrangements. The appeal of a beautifully dried arrangement in a display window, whose advantage of durability is obvious, has sold many pieces of china and linen, as well as other house furnishings.

YOUR FLOWER GARDEN MAY CHANGE

When you walk through your garden on a sunny afternoon admiring your choice roses, or the long spikes of stately delphinium, your pleasure is heightened by knowing that you can cut and process them by one of the methods described in this book. Your plant material, dried by these methods, will not shed, and will retain its color and shape for months, sometimes years. Dozens of varieties of flowers can be dried so perfectly that you need to reach out and touch them to make sure they are not fresh.

In the following pages you will find lists of plants that dry well and lastingly, also those that dry well but do not last, and those that do not respond successfully to any known drying method. Armed with this information, you can plant the flowers in your garden which you will want to dry as well as cut for fresh arrangements. You will scan the seed catalogues for new varieties of the everlastings, or those which the grower has labeled as good for drying. When choosing plants and seed, keep in mind the colors you enjoy most and, if you are thinking in terms of enhancing your home, those colors which you have used in your decorating schemes.

Blooms that dry best are those subjected to the best growing conditions. A plant grown in soil suited to its needs, well cultivated, provided with the correct type and amount of nourishment, moisture, and sunshine, will yield the best blossoms for drying. Oddly enough, the "last roses of summer" are frequently the prettiest and dry the best.

IF YOU ARE AN APARTMENT DWELLER

If you are a window-box gardener or if you must depend upon florists' flowers, this is all the more reason you should employ drying methods to capture and retain the beauty of your fresh blossoms. When you receive a gift of roses, glads, small mums, or stock from the greenhouse, keep out a few to dry. An increasing number of florists offer dried plants for sale, including the exotic tropical-date-palm embryos, the wood roses, ti leaves, fresh or dried, which look charming with fresh fruits, vegetables, or perhaps a few dried flowers.

Artificial flowers, sold today in department stores, have a fidelity of form and color to their fresh counterparts that is astonishing. Arrangements of these with glycerinized leaves or with artificial foliage can be made following the same principles outlined in Chapter VI for dried flowers. The mechanics that include containers and means of holding the plant material in place for dried flowers would certainly be adaptable for artificial flowers. Some of these are made of plastic, whereas others have a paper base coated with wax. While most flower lovers prefer nature's own bloom processed by one of the drying methods described in the following pages, these man-made plants artistically arranged are certainly in good taste. That they would not be acceptable in any kind of an exhibit of a horticultural nature is perfectly obvious, any more than painted or dyed materials could be used.

For the city dweller as well as for those with fragrant gardens, excursions into the countryside will yield an abundance of lovely plant material to dry. Along the roadside you will find such things as goldenrod, joe-pye weed, mullein, and many grasses. In the fields will be oxeye daisies, black-eyed Susans, rabbit tobacco, and dock, to mention only a few. If you are fortunate enough to attend a "county fair," you will find exhibits of prize-winning farm products which the owners may give you or sell for almost nothing. Many farmers are indulgent toward visitors who want to "borrow" some cornhusks and blades, a bit of bearded wheat, or a few stalks of millet.

What a pleasure it will be to saunter through the woods, even in winter, your eyes alert for the beauty of a bent twig, a curved root, a budding branch, or a subtly colored lichen inconspicuous against a tree trunk. In spring, summer, and fall your harvest of wild blossoms, leaves, seeds, cones, and berries will not outweigh the pleasure you have had in gathering them. As in the pursuit of any interest that takes you out of doors, probably your greatest reward will be a keener appreciation of nature's gifts. On that last fishing trip, for example, when the trout refused to bite, you might have filled your empty creel with milkweed pods, bramble berries, or ground cherries. Regardless of where you live, a perusal of these pages will suggest limitless sources of plant material for you to dry.

1. Subtle use of form and color makes this modern arrangement distinctive. Ti leaves establish the line of the design, while glycerinized magnolia leaves and seed cones frame the rosy pomegranate. The container has been painted to harmonize with the colors in the leaves.

HOW TO USE YOUR DRIED ARRANGEMENTS

You need not become bored by looking at the same arrangement for weeks on end. After a few days store that particular display under a large box on some shelf in a dry location, such as a closet or attic. (Not the basement, please, it might be damp!) Have another dried bouquet ready to take its place. You can interchange your dried materials, using the wood roses, magnolia leaves, and branches that you had in the living room, on a bamboo mat in the hall. Or if, after handling many times, your material becomes a bit tired-looking, it can be trimmed or sprayed a color—perhaps gold or white to be used later for some special occasion. What a pleasure at Christmas when you are so busy with the holiday rush to have a supply of leaves, cones, berries, all tinted and ready to make up into gay holiday decorations. Better yet, have the arrangements for the special day made up in advance so that all you have to do is to set them out!

Dust-catchers, you say? Dried arrangements can be dusted just as you would other furnishings in your home. For very delicate material, use a feather and a very light touch. A camel's-hair brush is sometimes suggested for heavier materials, whereas the glycerinized foliage can be wiped clean with a damp cloth or one dipped in mineral oil. Twigs and branches can be dusted with a cloth, and the container itself should be wiped clean when necessary.

Of course dried arrangements are more welcome in the winter and actually hold up better in a heated room. But even in summer when you are busy making every golden sunny hour count, a dried arrangement will be a joy, eliminating the necessity of replacing it every few days as you would with fresh flowers.

If you are not an expert arranger, you can experiment with your material until you have just the design you want, never fearing that it will wilt as you work. One word of caution: you will want to learn to cultivate a very light touch, for dried flowers are easily broken. But if you cut a stem too short, all is not lost, as it would be with fresh flowers, for you can lengthen a dried stem by one of the three methods described in this book. The result of your efforts with your new hobby will be a beautiful arrangement which has cost you nothing, will usually last for months, and requires very little attention.

The descriptions of methods of drying and the photographs of the arrangements in this book will be guideposts for you to carry out your own original ideas that may come with the reading of these pages. The beauty of flowers need not be fragmentary and fleeting but a lasting pleasure for you.

I I

Preparing a Place to Work

One distinct advantage of flower-drying as a hobby is the fact that it does not require expensive equipment. The cost of the materials needed in preserving plants is very slight compared to the hours of pleasure you will have in arranging and enjoying them in your home. Only a minimum of preparation is needed for drying flowers, but once you have started bringing in plant material to process, you will want everything in readiness.

Your work space must be *dry* and *warm*. An attic or closet is much more desirable than a basement, which may be damp. Bear in mind that moisture is your enemy during the preparation of your flowers for drying, during the drying period, and after the arrangement has been completed. Direct sunlight is to be avoided also, as light tends to fade your dried blossoms. A dry, not too light attic, inaccessible to the inquisitive hands of children and curious friends, would be ideal. You will be surprised at the number of adults who will almost unconsciously pick up a stalk of dried larkspur, breaking away a floret before you can caution them.

Photograph 2 shows the author's attic converted into a drying area. The exposed rafters have been utilized as drying racks by driving small nails a foot or so apart. Specific directions are given in Chapter IV for drying plants by hanging. The advantage here is that flowers can be placed for drying on the nails, then left there undisturbed until they are to be used in an arrangement. The arranger can find the color, shape, and size she wants by merely glancing over the collection. However, if they are apt to become dusty in the open, they can be stored in boxes protected from light and moisture by tight-fitting lids. Each box should be labeled with the name of the variety of flower, the quantity, and the date on which they were dried.

Some arrangers use a transparent plastic covering, such as Saran Wrap, instead of a lid for sealing out the moisture and easy visual identification of the flowers. Others in especially humid regions and during the summer months find it necessary to place crystals of some dehumidifier such as Dri-Rox in the box to absorb moisture. However, if any blossom is noticeably "droopy" while stored in a box, it will certainly droop in your arrangement and is not worth the time and effort of drying.

Not all houses these days have attics that can be used as a work space. In that case a closet or pantry could be used. Additional poles might be installed to hold clothes hangers, each of which would support several bunches of plants for drying. Taut wires or tightly stretched clotheslines would serve the same purpose. Boxes for storing your dried flowers would be safe on the closet shelves; heavy cartons holding sand for drying can be set on the floor. The kitchen table is still the old stand-by for most homemakers and serves well for preparing flowers and arranging them if separate space is not available.

2. An attic is an ideal location for storing dried-plant material, as it is usually warm, dry, and not too light. Nails driven into the rafters provide space for hanging bundles of plants to dry and to leave in storage.

Drying racks can be made if no attic or closet is handy. Mabel Squires, in her book *The Art of Drying Plants*, describes a circular rack made by installing two thirty-six-inch dowel pins radially on a discarded lamp base which supports bunches of dried flowers.

WHAT YOU WILL NEED

For the four principal drying methods described in this book, you will need the following supplies:

(a) For *sand-drying*, in which the flower head is actually buried during the drying period, you will want about half a "yard" of sand, depending on the amount of drying you plan to do. Actually this means about half a cubic yard of sand to those employed in the business of making concrete. Here in Virginia such an amount of sand would cost about fifty cents. Some gravel-supply businesses have sand-pile sand for children, which has been washed. Or you may be able to bring home a couple of bucketfuls on your next excursion to the lake or river. The sand of rivers or inland lakes is best, as it is not apt to contain foreign substances or chemicals found in salt-water sand. The latter can be well washed, however, and thoroughly dried and used for processing flowers.

Your sand must be extremely fine. Sifting is highly recommended to remove foreign particles. Dry your sand either by exposing it to the sun or to the heat of your oven.

Some successful flower driers use not only sand but a mixture of sand and borax, or borax alone. Others have experimented with cornstarch, powdered sugar, fuller's earth, alum, powdered pumice, corn meal, both white and yellow, to mention a few. The author relies entirely on fine, very dry sand to give the best results for these reasons: (1) it is cheaper; (2) it will not deteriorate and can be used indefinitely; (3) it does not attract insects; (4) most important, it falls away cleanly from your blossoms after it has done its work of drying. Your flower's color is fresh and without the dusty look it often has with borax or one of the powdery mixtures. Many borax users complain of having to brush their dried blossoms to remove the borax, or even to resort to passing them under water to get a clean look. If you use sand alone, all this is unnecessary. The drying time for sand averages about four days for most flowers, no longer than if borax or a combination had been used.

If you think that insects might attack your drying flowers—and they will if any are around!—combine a small amount of borax with the sand, say half a cup to a cubic foot of sand. This will not be enough to affect the appearance of your flowers but will act only as an insect repellent. Precaution is to be noted for mice as well; dried flowers seem to be a favorite food with them!

You will need a heavy cardboard carton strong enough to support sand about four inches deep and of sufficient surface to accommodate

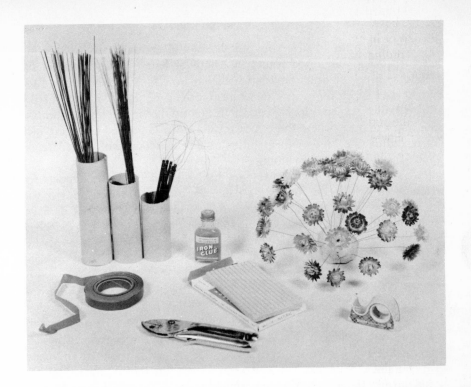

3. The equipment necessary for drying and arranging dried flowers is quite meager. Clay has many uses; here it holds a group of strawflowers during their drying period. It is also used in preparing the container to hold flowers. Clippers and florist's wire, tape and wooden picks all help to make the processes of drying and arranging easier.

several flowers. A carton six to eight inches deep and two feet wide by three feet long would be convenient. However, if you do not have space for this large a container, a smaller one of the same depth will do, or several small boxes might be more satisfactory for your use. A wooden box is not practical, as it will leak sand through its cracks. There is also danger of catching splinters in your fingernails as you work.

A pair of sturdy clippers is indispensable for all drying methods. You will want them with you on trips to the woods, or to your garden to cut plant stems, as well as during the preparation of your specimens for drying, and in the actual arranging.

Florist's wire is used in drying of several types of blossoms such as roses, strawflowers, and globe amaranth, to mention a few. Buy a supply of three sizes: No. 18, No. 22, and No. 26. The largest is used for artificial stems, the medium-sized wire for grouping and tying, and the smallest, finest wire is needed occasionally in making the arrangement. Fifty cents should purchase an abundance of each.

You will want to save your suit boxes and cartons with good-fitting lids for storing your dried plants. A length of Saran Wrap is handy for sealing a carton of dried flowers which has no lid. A supply of Dri-Rox, as mentioned before, or any moisture-absorbing crystals, to place in the storage boxes to keep dried flowers dry is helpful during the humid summer months or in areas where there is excess moisture. Gummed labels are nice for recording the kinds and quantity of flowers along with the date on which they were placed in storage.

(b) For *hanging* your flowers to dry, you will need the clippers for cutting and defoliaging, perhaps a paper bag or folds of newsprint if you are a distance from home for transporting plant material without damage. At home you will need twine or heavy florist's wire to hold it in bunches. Some flower driers use pipe cleaners or "plas-ties," which is a plastic-covered wire for this purpose. And, of course, you need a dry, not-too-light place to hang and store them.

(c) For processing in *glycerine*: a supply of glycerine—cheaper if you can buy it in bulk rather than by the bottle—water, a small-mouthed bottle, and a hammer for pounding woody stems. Your glycerinizing foliage need not be placed in a dark, dry area during the processing period. Indeed, the green leaves can grace your den or family room in an attractive container. This way you can keep an eye on the absorption of the glycerine into the leaves. Also you can add water as the solution evaporates.

(d) For *pressing*, you will want newsprint with short lengths of lumber, or large books for weighting the foliage. And, of course, an area to accommodate the press where it will not be disturbed.

WHAT TO DRY AND WHERE TO FIND IT

Plant material to dry can be found everywhere. The roadside will yield grasses and pods. The woods hold treasures of twisted roots and oddly shaped branches, colorful leaves and berries. The fields, the farm, the bank of the river, and your own back yard will become unlimited sources of material for you to dry.

With experience your eye will become trained to see beauty where beauty did not exist for you before. A new awareness of the marvels of nature is an additional reward for the person who seeks beauty out of doors. You will notice that even the humblest roadside grasses change their appearance with the seasons, and by drying them at different stages of their development, you will have an abundant supply of material. Many plants such as wheat, oats, and barley should be cut at different times during their growing season, resulting in dried specimens that range in color from pale green to rich mellow gold.

WHEN TO HARVEST PLANT MATERIAL

In the fall, Mother Nature does the work of drying plant material for you. Seed pods, stalks of grain, and other attractive foliage can be plucked already dried and ready to store or use in an arrangement. Thanksgiving designs made of material matured and dried by nature are especially appropriate. The colors are mainly brown, some almost mahogany, such as ripe dock (also called curly dock or sour dock), shading into the beiges. Look for the tassels of sweet or field corn, which are almost white.

Milk-weed pods can be plucked after they have dried on the stalk, when their seeds have been shed. Remember, too, that they can be cut while green, forced open, the seeds removed, and dried to a lovely pale green with yellow centers. More about this in the chapter on hanging plants to dry.

If you live in the Mid-Western plains region, you will be familiar with the tall spikelike flowers of the yucca plant. In the fall after the seeds

4. Spring has come to stay in this low, green bowl with its perfectly dried daffodils, bells-of-Ireland, pussy willow, and cattail foliage.

have scattered, you can cut these spikes with their attractive pods. These need to be hung inverted for four or five days to dry any moisture that may be left in the thick stalk.

Late in the fall the seed heads of many plants empty their loads of seeds, but withstand the effects of rain, sleet, even snow, to become bleached to a creamy white. Indeed, all through the winter you will find interestingly weathered stalks, seed pods, and calyxes, whose subtle coloring will add distinction to your arrangement.

As winter progresses and boughs of trees are bared to view, you will find on your tramps through the woods interestingly bent twings, branches, and exposed roots that are not obvious in the summer. Bits of driftwood, weathered and bleached, may be found along the banks of rivers and lakes. The cones of some of the conifers drop in late winter and early spring. You will want to gather these from the trees while they are fresh and clean.

Early spring brings the furry budding of the pussy willow and cattails growing in wet areas along lake beds. Gather pussy willow when the soft gray buds are pushing out of the branch and place them in an empty jar to dry.

Flowering branches of the forsythia, many fruit-tree blossoms, japonica, and bridal wreath can be dried beautifully in spring. This is the time to pick the early-blooming jonquils and narcissus for drying. The foliage of these two flowers is too moist and tender for drying. However, cattail leaves are very similar to those of narcissus and jonquils, or you can use the foliage of iris or gladiolus.

Summertime, with its burst of blossoming colors and forms, offers an infinite variety for your choice of flowers to dry. The early-blooming perennials and annuals in your garden will probably keep you and your drying racks busy. However, it is well to be prepared whenever you are away from home by having your clippers handy, and empty bottles or tin cans in your car for bouquets you want to bring home to dry. Oasis, or "unspillable water," is a plastic brick that holds moisture and your flower stems while transporting them. Folds of newsprint are handy for fern fronds or other foliage that can be dried by pressing.

There is a complete list of plant material for drying in the end papers of this book with the correct drying method for each. There may be plants not listed here, plants native to your regions, which will be well worth a try at drying.

There is no limit to the source of plant material which you will find suitable for your dried arrangements.

5. A ten-cent-store glass vase, painted a dull gray and placed on a small teakwood base, becomes a charming container for a Hogarth curve arrangement. Silvery artemisia outlines the curve, which is filled in with poppy pods, roses, and pressed rose leaves.

III

Sand-Drying

❦ This simple way of drying flowers may be the most practical and rewarding method you will try. When a blossom has been correctly placed in sand, each petal carefully supported in its original position, absorption of the flower's moisture will be uniform and gradual during the drying period. When you remove it from the sand, you will find that it has retained its shape and color to a remarkable degree. Best of all, it will remain in excellent condition for months and sometimes years.

As was stated in the preceding chapter, many mixtures have been tried as drying agents. But after experimenting with a number of these, the authors have found that sand alone is most satisfactory.

Your sand must be very fine, clean, dry, and preferably fresh-water sand. Sifting is recommended to remove coarse grains and foreign particles. For this you might use a discarded flour sifter or a piece of wire screening. The box that holds the sand should be strong, deep enough to support about four inches of sand, and of sufficient area to accommodate several blossoms drying at once. The box should not be moved after the flowers have been put in for drying.

DRYING ROSES

The rose, favorite of so many flower lovers, dries beautifully in sand. The instructions for drying roses can be applied to many other flowers similar in structure, such as carnations, small dahlias, the florets of delphinium, gladiolus, and hollyhock. If carefully followed, these directions will give beautiful results.

Suppose you have in your garden a small, partially opened rose, perhaps a Fashion. Cut it with a very short stem. Actually you will want it only one-fourth to one-half inch long when you prepare it for drying. Do this during the driest time of the day, usually in the afternoon when no dew is present to hinder the absorption of the flower's moisture. Be ready to put the rose into sand immediately, as you do not want it to wilt. Frequently beautiful blossoms are spoiled by insect damage. Aphids and other pests reduce the vitality of the plant and make its blooms poor specimens for drying. Regular spraying of your rose bushes will keep them free of insects. Be careful not to spray the rose itself, as it will be spotted or stained by the chemicals in the spray. The leaves of the bush can be washed to remove any residual deposits of the spray before pressing them.

Insert a heavy florist's wire (No. 18) into the cut end of the stem and push it well up into the hard green base of the rose, called the calyx (see Figure 1). After your rose has been dried, it will cling to the wire stem, which can then be cut with your clippers to any length or bent in any curve that you might want. When the natural stem has been left on the rose during the drying period, it will be stiff, brittle, and often awkwardly bent. By wiring your stem first you will avoid damaging the blossom when handling it later. Also, if you cut the rose with a very short stem, you will not destroy undeveloped buds left on the plant as you would if you were to cut a long stem.

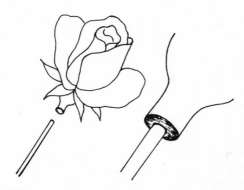

Figure 1. To prepare a rose for sand-drying, trim the stem of the rose to one-fourth inch and insert a florist's wire into the cut end of the stem.

It is most important that you place your bloom correctly in the sand so that no petal is turned or crushed during the process.

Bend the wire stem on the rose at right angles close to the head of the flower. This may be an inch or so from the calyx. This permits the wire stem to rest in the sand out of the way after the rose is in position for drying.

With your hand, scoop away a small amount of sand to form a depression on the surface. Place the rose, head up, in this depression, its wire stem imbedded in the sand. Now gently press the sand in and around the outside of the rose, forming a wall of sand against the outer petals of the rose, supporting them in their original positions.

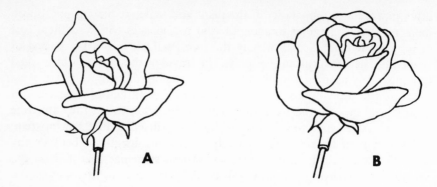

Figure 2. Not all varieties of roses dry well. Choose those with short uncurled petals as in b. Roses whose petals curl, as in a, are difficult to put in sand.

Next, scoop a little sand into your hand and allow it to trickle from your closed palm in a fine stream around each petal. Allow the sand to build up equally on all sides of each petal so that its position is not altered. Start with the outer petals and work inward row by row. By the time you have reached the center, the rose will have disappeared, each petal surrounded and supported in sand. If you see that petals are bending under the influx of sand, you are probably permitting too much sand to descend from your hand, or the pressure may be uneven on one side of the petal. Narrow your stream of sand and sift it around the petal, making sure it builds up equally on all sides.

You will find that sifting the sand around the petals is not difficult, and with practice your dexterity will increase. The reward is a beautifully dried rose, almost perfect in shape and color.

If you think you may forget where each rose is buried, sift a small mound of sand over the area where you have placed the blossom.

In normal weather, roses should be dry in about four days. It is best to test one petal by brushing aside some of the sand carefully with the tip of your finger. If the petal feels crisp and dry, you may take the rose out, admire it, and place it carefully in a box for storage. A strong suit box or carton with a closely fitting lid would be good for this. Label the box with the name of the rose, the date on which it was stored, and the number of blossoms in the box at that time. This will save opening your boxes and searching for the needed blossoms later when you start your arrangement.

If the weather is damp, you may leave your flowers in the sand until the atmosphere is drier. Always make every effort to keep dampness away from dried flowers.

A rose that has been allowed to mature on the bush and is completely open is apt to lose its shape after it is dried, due to the absorption of moisture in the air. However, if you have such a rose, it can be dried. When you bring it in from the garden, trim the stem to half an inch or less, and wire it as described. Hold it in your left hand, circling your thumb and index finger around it, drawing in the petals. Press it gently into the sand with your right forefinger against the soft feathery center of the rose. Sift sand carefully around and between the petals as previously described, until it is just covered in sand. Take a very open rose out of the sand after a day or two, or before it is completely dry, and hang it to finish drying. If it is left in the sand too long, the petals may shatter. When this happens, all may not be lost, for with patience you can glue the petals back in place. Put a small amount of glue—any that is suitable for porous materials —on the inner edge of the petal and press it to the place where it separated from the rose. Hold it a few minutes until the glue has set. When it is dry, place it in a box for storage.

6. To sand-dry a rose, first scoop away a small amount of sand, forming a slight depression. Let the rose nestle there, its artificial wire stem extending below the surface of the sand. Scoop a small amount of sand in your hand and allow it to trickle in a fine stream around the petals of the rose.

DRYING ROSEBUDS

Rosebuds are especially charming in dried arrangements. Their spike-like forms are helpful in your design and they lend a natural and delicate look to the arrangement. You should dry buds that are showing some color in the tips, as well as tight, all-green ones. These are left on their natural stems, as the stems will not be bent. With the side of your hand, make a shallow trough in the sand and lay the rosebuds horizontally in the depression. Sift sand over them and leave them at least four days or until they are dry. Test them for crispness, and if they are dry, store them in a box.

For more developed rosebuds, with a petal or two unfurled, handle as you would a partially open rose. That is, trim the stems to half an inch or less and wire them. Then place the flower heads up in sand and carefully sift sand around them. Test them for dryness after four days. The large buds of the hybrid tea roses should be tested after three or four days. If the outer petals are crisp, remove them from the sand and hang them to allow the heavy centers to dry. Your bud will be prettier than if you had left it in sand for the entire time.

When a more open rosebud is desired, you may hold it close to your mouth and blow into it until the petals have loosened and spread a little. Fill it with sand while it is cupped in your hand. Then place it head up in the sand and sift sand very carefully around it.

WHAT COLORS DRY BEST?

Although the color of your dried flower is beautiful, it may not be exactly the same shade it was when fresh. Some flowers dry a trifle darker than the original color and often there is a slight graying. This does not detract from its beauty, but you may find that blossoms which blended before drying do not go well together after drying. The opposite, of course, is also true; some dried materials often harmonize better than they would have before they were processed.

In general, light colors are more useful to the arranger, as dark shades tend to recede to the observer and sometimes cause a visual void, or "hole," in the arrangement. In selecting roses, use shades of pink, yellow, and white, preferably.

WHAT VARIETIES OF ROSES DRY BEST?

Choose varieties of small roses with short, uncurled petals (see Figure 2). It is very hard to sift sand around a petal that has curled, as it is apt to bend and dry in an awkward position. Large roses do not dry as well as smaller ones. Also their broad petals are apt to absorb moisture after they are processed. When they are used in an arrangement they may droop.

As a general rule, the floribundas dry best. Talisman roses dry well, but they "gray" slightly in the process. When you cut your roses, pick some rose leaves and press them between the pages of a book, as described in Chapter V.

The following are some of the roses that dry with excellent results.

MA PERKINS: dries to a delicate pink
LILLIBET: similar to Ma Perkins
CORAL PILLAR: pinker than Lillibet
FASHION: dries to a salmon pink
BETTER TIMES: about the deepest red you can use, nice with deep-red crested cockscomb
VOGUE: dries to a deep rose
DIAMOND JUBILEE: yellow with a rosy center
PINOCCHIO: similar to Ma Perkins
CHARLOTTE ARMSTRONG: deep-rose color
PINK BOUNTIFUL: orchid pink with nice straight petals

OTHER FLOWERS DRIED LIKE ROSES

Asters, dried by the method just described, are very lovely, but delicate to handle. Little pompon dahlias retain their color and form for years. All colors of these charming flowers dry well, but the lighter colors may be more useful to you. The florets of delphinium, gladiolus, and hollyhock can be wired and placed in the sand, heads up, and dried just as you do roses. Carnations are handled in the same way.

DRYING LARKSPUR

Larkspur dries to unbelievable perfection. When it emerges from the sand, its colors are as clear and delicate as when it was fresh. Grow an abundance of this lovely flower in all its shades of blue, pink, and white, for you will find many uses for it in arrangements.

Pick the spike of larkspur while it has unopened buds at the end: that is, before it has bloomed out completely. Its form will be more pointed and delicate, and more useful in giving outline to your design. Most arrangements are more pleasing if round shapes are combined with spike shapes, and frequently these are hard to find. Cut the larkspur during the driest time of the day, before the evening dew has condensed on them. This rule holds for all flowers intended for drying. Snip the leaves from the stem immediately, but do not cut away the stem as with the rose.

Make an elongated, troughlike depression on the sand, and place the larkspur lengthwise in this depression. Some florets will be face down,

7. A crescent arrangement, glowing with color, has been constructed on a silver bread tray. Silvery artemisia outlines the design, filled in with larkspur, xeranthemum, statice, cockscomb, and bits of hydrangea. The lovely color and perfect form of the roses, violas, and pansies are achieved by careful sand-drying.

others up, some turned to the side. Starting with the bottom floret on the spike, the one facing down, sift sand very slowly and carefully around the little flower. In this manner a wall of sand is built up, and the flower does not change its original position. Move on to the next blossom facing down, and let the stream of sand from your hand form a wall around it as you did with the first.

Now cover the florets facing the sides, by sifting sand alternately on each side. As the wall of sand grows, the little flower is held in its original position. Finally, the floret facing up can be covered with sand sifted carefully around the petals just as the rose was covered. Proceed in this manner up the length of the stalk until the entire spike of the larkspur is covered with sand.

Throughout this process be very careful not to rush your sand-sifting, as sand poured too rapidly will crumple your blossom.

In ordinary weather, larkspur will be dry in four days. You will want a large collection of these beautiful spike-shaped flowers in all their lovely colors, as they are so useful and dry as well as any flower you will try.

DRYING DELPHINIUM

Delphinium, like larkspur, dries exceptionally well. Cut the smaller side shoots rather than the central stalk to dry in the same manner as larkspur. If the main stalk is too large to dry as a spike and to use later in an arrangement, cut the individual florets from the stalk. These are then dried heads up in sand as you would roses. They can be used individually or grouped in an arrangement.

Many of the improved hybrid double varieties of delphinium retain their color and shape to an amazing degree when they are dried in sand. The brighter shades of blue delphinium with the white center, or "bee," as it is sometimes called, are more useful to the arranger than those with the dark "bee." When flowers of the darker shades of any color are used in an arrangement and viewed from a distance, they seem to recede, and tend to leave a void, or "hole," in the arrangement.

OTHER FLOWERS DRIED LIKE LARKSPUR

Snapdragons, when dried, retain their color well. Some arrangers hang snapdragons to dry, but their shape is much more natural if they are dried in sand. Chinese forget-me-nots are especially pretty dried in sand, and provide a beautiful blue, sometimes hard to find. Buddleia, or the butterfly bush, and lupine are processed the same way. As the stem of a spike of lupine is hollow, you may push a medium-sized florist's wire (No. 22) up through the stem and shape it into the curve you want for your arrangement before drying.

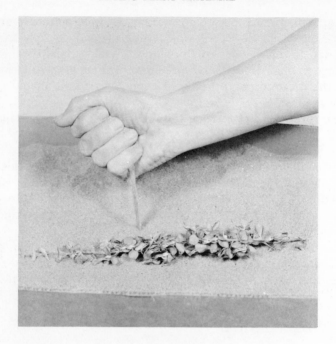

8. To sand-dry larkspur, place the stalk horizontally on the sand in a slight depression which you have made with your hand. Then sift a fine stream of sand in and around the individual florets until each is covered.

Canadian lilac, the variety which dries best, holds its shape well, but the color sometimes becomes dull in the drying process. However, it is useful as a filler.

Bells-of-Ireland are especially useful for their lovely green color—a shade hard to find in flowers. Some authors suggest hanging these interesting flowers to dry, but this results in their delicate tips withering and drying unattractively. If they are placed in sand in the same way in which you dry larkspur, their color will be greener and fresher-looking. The tender green tips can be dried just as naturally as the lower part of the stalk. You may want more curve to the bells-of-Ireland. This can be obtained by placing the fresh spray on a needle holder at an angle and allowing it to stand in very shallow water, just enough water to keep the cut end of the stalk wet. The stem of the flower will curve upward in a few hours, or overnight at the most. Then it can be placed in the sand box for drying.

If you prefer, you can push a medium-weight wire (No. 22) into the hollow stem of the bells-of-Ireland while it is fresh, and bend it into the curve you need.

9. Larkspur, perfectly dried in sand, retains its delicate form and color to an amazing degree. Here, a design of beautiful blue, pink, and white larkspur frames a collection of roses and daisies, also sand-dried. An appropriate container for this magnificent array is the charming silver stand placed on a reflecting mirror.

10. These graceful bells-of-Ireland have been sand-
dried, preserving their delicate color and form. They
blend with the green pottery bowl, the darker green
of the glycerinized ivy leaves, and the marigolds,
which have dark green centers.

Spears of the smallest varieties of gladioli, which have only three or
four opened florets, can be very successfully dried in sand. Cover them
with sand as you would larkspur, but watch for opening florets that will
bloom out under the sand. As these opening blooms push out, you will
want to cover them with sand to dry. As with most flowers, choose the
lighter colors and dry an abundance, as some will hold up perfectly whereas others of the same variety may not. Test the flowers described in this
section in four days, with the exception of the last, gladioli, which should
be allowed to remain in the sand a few days longer. As gladiolus stalks are
moist and fleshy, they require a week of normal weather to be thoroughly
dry. You can cut single florets from the stem and wire them as you would
roses, drying them in sand, heads up.

DRYING ZINNIAS

When selecting zinnias to dry, as with any flower, choose the straight-
petaled varieties rather than the new, curled, fringed ones. The rule about
color still holds: not too dark!

Trim the leaves from the stem, but leave the stem *long*. The head of the zinnia is placed *down* on the sand. Taking the stem in your left hand (if you are right-handed), hold the flower face lightly against the sand and with your right hand sift sand carefully around the outer petals of the blossom. Circle the stream of sand row by row around the zinnia until the entire flower head is covered.

The stem will dry, drooping to the sand, producing a nice curve. When you remove the dried flower, it will face out, not up, in your arrangement. If the stem has dried sturdily and is long enough, it will need no other support.

Oddly enough, one variety of zinnia, called Linearis, dries to a brighter color than the fresh flower. It is a small single-petaled flower of a clear orange color. The dried Linearis simply glows—almost a flame color! Very useful in arrangements also are the little pompon zinnias, and the Lilliput, or carpet zinnia. You will probably find more opportunities to use these smaller, paler-colored zinnias than the big, darker-colored ones.

11.   To dry a zinnia in sand, place it gently with its flower head down in a slight depression in the sand. Sift sand slowly around the zinnia until it is covered with sand.

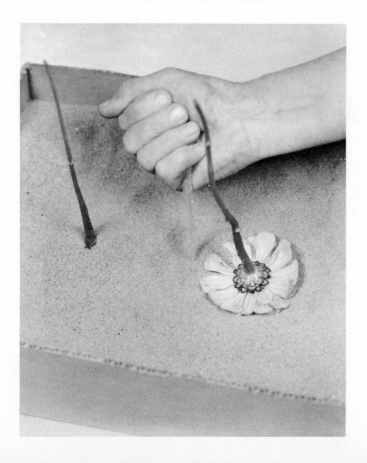

12. An elegant alabaster container holds an equally elegant array of delphinium, gladioli, and roses. A cluster of artificial grapes blends in color and texture with the entire composition. Notice the rosebuds and leaves which have been dried in sand along with the rest of the plant material.

13. The gray tones of this pewter container blend with the gray-green of the Queen Anne's lace and the orchid of the zinnias. The delicate spikes of henbane (*Hyoscyamus niger*) are also gray in color and resemble small bells. Bits of hydrangea were used as filler.

OTHER FLOWERS DRIED LIKE ZINNIAS

The plain little field daisies, called oxeye daisies, which you see along the roadside and sprinkled across the fields, dry wonderfully well. For a spot of pure white, so natural and refreshing in your arrangement, use these dainty straight-petaled flowers, dried heads down with wire stems in sand like zinnias. Another charmer from the fields is the black-eyed Susan, which dries wonderfully well in the same manner. Shasta daisies dry well, too, but their larger petals provide more area for absorption of moisture and are apt to droop in humid weather.

Ageratum, dried like zinnias, emerges from the sand the same beautiful blue that it was when fresh. It can be hung to dry, but sand-drying preserves its feathery shape and clear-blue color.

14. This deep container displays a crescent whose outline is made of larkspur. Pompon dahlias, which dry so perfectly in sand, are used as filler, while roses and pressed rose leaves become the center of interest.

Marigolds are dried heads down in sand, similar to daisies and zinnias. However, the center of the marigold is heavy and moist, and it may turn dark and rot or mold. To prevent this, when the outer petals of the marigold have dried, take the flower out of the sand and hang it by a string tied to the stem to finish drying.

Peonies should also be dried heads up in sand, then removed and hung to finish drying as soon as the outer petals are crisp. The round buds of peonies which show a little color can be dried in the same manner and are charming in arrangements.

Pansies can be dried either with their pretty faces up or down in the sand.

Lantana, nigella, and bachelor's-buttons are handled the same as zinnias.

FLOWERS THAT DRY WELL BUT DO NOT LAST

Some flowers can be successfully dried in sand, but retain their color and shape for only a few months. The effort involved in processing them, however, is often worth while.

Jonquils and narcissus dried as you would roses, heads up in sand, will hold up for a month or two. The trumpets or centers should be carefully filled with sand before placing them in the box for drying.

Tulips, small ones that are not too open, hold up very well, but in time their petals are apt to droop or fall off. Tulips and some lilies, such as the lemon lily, can be dried by first holding the blossom in your hand and filling it carefully with sand. Then place it in a depression in the sand, stem down, at an angle—in a rather reclining position. Thus the head of the flower will be supported while you sift sand around the petals. The Easter lily will hold up, surprisingly enough, for a much longer period of time than any other lilies.

The florets of hollyhocks will hold up for a while if you choose small blossoms that are not too open. The white and pale-pink hollyhocks are especially pretty, but dark varieties will dry even darker and are not usually useful. Trim the stems of the florets to half an inch or less and insert a heavy florist's wire up through the cut end into the hard green calyx, and place these heads up in sand. Dry the short stalks of this flower while there are green buds at the end and a bloom or two at the bottom, for a lovely addition to your arrangement. Place the hollyhock stalk on the sand lengthwise and cover with sand as you would a spike of larkspur.

Sweet rocket may fade after a month or two, but its rich color will be a pleasure for a time. Even dogwood blooms can be preserved and enjoyed for a while. Apple blossoms, though they do not last long, are reward enough for their fragile beauty.

Even sunflowers can be dried, if you select the small side blooms of the large flowered varieties. Do not expect them to last more than a few months.

Always dry more material than you will need, for some blooms may not process as you might expect. Many conditions of weather during the drying, as well as the elements surrounding the growing flower, affect its ability to hold up after it has been dried.

SAND-DRYING LEAVES

Small leaves can also be dried in sand. If the axial leaves on the stalk of your blossom are small, such as the second bloom of sunflowers, leave one or two on the stalk. This violates the paramount rule to defoliage as soon as the flower is cut, but in a few cases where the flower head faces

15. These sunflowers have been sand-dried and arranged in a wooden compote. The brown glycerinized magnolia leaves blend perfectly with the mullein stalk, which has gone to seed.

out and not up, it can be dried stalk, leaves, and all in sand. Place the sun-flower with one or two of the leaves nearest the bloom face down on a depression in the sand, its stem lying horizontally on the sand. Sift sand until bloom, stalk, and leaves are all covered. You will want to test leaves and flower petals after four days.

One or two leaves nearest the bud of a rose can be left on the stem and dried in the same way.

Photograph 16 shows three sprays of ivy which have been dried in sand. These were chosen for their graceful curves and were cut to fit to-gether to form the design for the arrangement. The three sprays were then laid on the sand horizontally and sifted with sand until they were covered, as you would a stalk of larkspur.

More time is required for thorough drying of the ivy stem and leaves than for blossoms. When drying conditions are ideal, it may take ten days to two weeks. Test the edges of the leaves as you would flower petals.

Sand-drying gives by far the most natural-looking dried-plant material. You may want to experiment on other flowers and foliage not mentioned in this chapter. For best results, remember to select small, straight-petaled, light-colored blossoms.

16. Three gracefully curved boughs of ivy were dried in sand, result-ing in fresh, clear color and perfect form. Arranged in a green pottery bowl, they are simple in design yet very effective.

IV

Drying Plants by Hanging

🜨 Drying plants by hanging is the method most widely used by flower arrangers today as it was in the past. Many plants retain their color and shape remarkably well by this simple method, and further treatment would be superfluous. Indeed, you will find that hanging some plants to dry is preferable to sand-drying. You may also want to try a new product called Silica Gel, an absorbing agent in which the flower head is completely immersed. While the results are good, the colors are bright and clear, it is quite expensive. Sand gives the same if not better results and is less costly.

Delightful bouquets can be made using materials dried by hanging alone. However, your variety and selection will be wider if you have materials dried by hanging, in sand, processed in glycerine, and pressed between newsprint.

As stated previously, the place in which you hang your flowers should be dry, warm, and not too light. If an attic is inaccessible, an infrequently used closet or pantry might serve to hold bunches of material. Avoid basements, porches, or garages, where dampness may creep in and ruin your specimens.

Materials included in this chapter are the everlastings, or immortelles, aromatic herbs, annuals, perennials, shrubs, roadside and farm materials, pods, nuts, and berries.

All plants to be dried should be defoliaged immediately after cutting, as the principle behind all drying is to dehydrate them as quickly as possible. Leaves left on the stem will contribute their moisture to the stalk as they dry, prolonging the drying period. Also, if the foliage remains on the stem, it will wither and must be removed before the flower can be used. This is more easily accomplished when the leaves are fresh.

Divide your plant material into small bunches to avoid crowding or crushing. The stems of the flowers are tied together with twine or a small cord. Some arrangers use wire, pipe cleaners, rubber bands, but anything will do that will hold them securely, and not cut or break the stems. Hang them heads down from nails spaced far enough apart to allow free circulation of air. The nails need only be large enough to hold your material,

17.   This antique crock oven dish has a gleaming dark-brown interior, similar
to the color of the glycerinized magnolia leaves. The gladiolus seed pods, dock,
and yellow cockscomb blend with the dull tan exterior of the dish.

and may be driven into the rafters of your attic or along the wall of a
closet. In the event that you have no space to drive nails, hang your bundles of plant material from coat hangers suspended from a crossbar.

The cord or twine should be drawn tightly so that the stems, when
they have dried and shrunk, will not slip from the bundles; yet it should
not be taut enough to cut or crush the stems.

In normal weather, grasses and lightweight plants should be dry in
about one week, while heavier materials may take two weeks or longer.
Leave the bundles hanging if they are free from dust and the space is not
needed. Or store them loosely in closed cartons, being careful not to crush
them. Label your boxes, giving the date, kind, and quantity of flowers
enclosed.

If a curved stem is desired, it may be placed in an empty jar while
drying. If the stem is upright, the weight of the flower head will cause it
to arch gracefully. A heavy pitcher will insure a nice curve if the flower
stem droops over the spout. A wide-mouthed vase should serve the same
purpose.

Large rough materials will require a container with sufficient weight and height to keep it from overturning.

Some flowers have such fragile stems that they must be replaced by wire while the flower is fresh. This is true of strawflowers and globe amaranth, but they must be dried in the air, not in sand. It would be awkward to try to hang these wire stems to dry. Instead the wire stems can be thrust into a ball of clay or even into a potato in such a way as to hold the flower heads apart during the drying process.

EVERLASTINGS

There is a group of flowers listed in seed catalogues as everlastings; the name is derived from their lasting qualities due to the unique stiffness of their petals. These are easy to grow and they dry beautifully by hanging. Their rich colors and interesting forms are very useful in arrangements.

Strawflowers, or Helichrysum, as they are listed, are well known as a favorite everlasting. They range in color from brilliant crimson through rose, salmon, yellow, and white. Some of these blooms reach two and a half inches in diameter. However, the smaller varieties are usually more useful. They are nice in your fresh arrangements, too.

Strawflowers should be picked in the bud and allowed to open as they dry. The dried stems of these flowers are not strong enough to hold their original positions, and the head will droop after it has been placed in the arrangements a few weeks. It is best, while they are fresh, to remove the stems and insert a florist's wire into each calyx, as is illustrated with the rose in Figure 1. When the bloom dries, it will adhere tightly to the wire. You can thrust several of the wire stems of these flowers into a ball of clay or into a potato. This will allow each blossom ample room in which to open and dry. After about two weeks, the flowers may be removed and stored in a large covered cardboard carton, labeled with date, kind, and quantity. If you have a large number, it is helpful to store them according to their colors.

Globe amaranth is an everlasting that resembles the common clover. The flower head is about three fourths of an inch across, and blooms in shades of purple, lavender, rose, pink, and white. This flower will give variety and form to your dried arrangement, as well as lovely color. Pick this flower when it is *fully* developed and replace its stem with wire. It can be used in an arrangement immediately or stored because it is stiff and dry as soon as it has reached maturity.

Xeranthemum is an everlasting with a charming, silky little bloom in shades of white, rose, and purple. Gather these flowers *at the peak of their bloom* for drying, and tie them in small bunches, hanging heads down to dry. In normal weather they should be dry after a week.

Another everlasting is statice. The variety Sinuata is good for drying. It blooms into tiny florets along a stem that springs horizontally from the

18. This modern container is made of tin funnels graduated in size. Bronze strawflowers describe a graceful line filled with achillea, ground cherries, milk-weed pods, and pomegranates. The grapes are artificial. Bearded wheat gives the whole composition a light, airy quality.

19. Antiques lend themselves beautifully as containers of old-fashioned bouquets. Here an old toothbrush holder, graceful and elegant in spite of its practical function, now displays larkspur, roses, strawflowers, silky little xeranthemum, and white statice.

main stem. It is especially useful in dried arrangements for its delicacy and exquisite colors. Statice should be picked at its fullest bloom, tied in small bunches, and dried hanging with heads down. It can be used about two weeks later.

Helipterum is a less-known everlasting, and blossoms into clusters of tiny yellow flowers. It should be *picked at the height of bloom*, and hung in small bunches to dry. However, if it is left on the plant too long before harvesting, it will shatter.

Honesty, or the money plant, is considered an everlasting. While its flowers are rather inconspicuous, its seed pods are large, silvery-looking discs about the size of a silver dollar. Gather the pods with long stems as soon as the seeds have loosened, indicating that they have reached maturity. Hang them with the seed pods down. If the seeds and their covers do not drop off during the two-week drying period, remove them, being careful not to damage the parchment-like membranes in the center.

OTHER FLOWERS DRIED BY HANGING

Celosia, sometimes called "cockscomb," is especially beautiful when dried by this method. It is almost indispensable to the arranger of dried flowers, for its varieties range in color from the richest magenta through the palest shades of pink as well as a deep gold to the lightest yellow-green.

20.   A gay wall plaque which will brighten your kitchen or breakfast nook can be made on an asbestos pad. Strawflowers, statice, cockscomb, and brightly colored bayberries give the design its color, while bits of hydrangea and goldenrod are used for contrast. Nandina leaves finish the outline. All of this lightweight material can be glued to the pad.

21.   The fine texture of alabaster requires the delicacy of fine-textured blossoms. Stately delphinium rises to regal heights above the statice, strawflowers, cockscomb, and pressed rose leaves.

Cockscomb is easily grown from seed and requires little care, but demands a good rich soil with plenty of sun and water.

The blooms of some varieties of cockscomb spread into wide fans or crests, while others are feather-tipped or "plumed," as they are sometimes called. Both the crested and the plumed can be grown either in the dwarf or tall varieties. The large velvety heads may be used as they are or broken into the size needed for a particular spot in your arrangement. Although it is an old-fashioned flower, new varieties are being developed all the time, varieties that may prove even more useful to the arranger. Dry these by tying them in small bunches, and hang heads down. Since the stalk is thick, this plant will require about three weeks in normal weather to dry.

Achillea is a favorite when dried for either the line or mass arrangement. The variety Golden Plate is the one to choose. It is a tall perennial, very attractive in your garden. Each stem is crowned with a large flat cluster of buttercup yellow. When the flowers are fully developed, cut them for drying and hang them in small bunches, heads down. They will be ready to use or store in about two weeks. Despite its sturdy qualities, achillea will blend perfectly with your more delicate flowers. If you prefer, you may arrange the fresh achillea, after you cut it, in a dry container and enjoy it while it dries. You will find that achillea will not droop or alter in form.

Some of the flowers in our grandmothers' gardens are not widely grown today. One of these especially lovely when dried by hanging is the lady's-finger. It blooms into tiny florets on a drooping spike in deep shades of rose. However, after drying about two weeks with its flower head down, the lady's-finger will be a straight spike, especially useful in arranging. It has a delicacy of form and color which blends well with the choicest garden flowers.

The little Japanese iris has two blooms on each stem. After the two buds of these blooms form, one opens a few days before the other. Pick these when the first bud has bloomed and the second is still unopened. Break off and discard the first bloom, then dry the second while it is still a tight bud. Hang the iris heads down in small bundles. After a week or so you will have an interesting flower form especially pretty for outline in your arrangement.

Gather boughs of bridal wreath when the small white blooms have opened, but before they have begun to shatter. Hang them inverted to dry. After about two weeks you will have a creamy white spike to add to your collection.

Hydrangea is a popular shrub whose large blossoms dry nicely by hanging. Leave the white variety of hydrangea, often listed as Hills of Snow, on the bush until it turns a pale green. Oddly enough, this stage is reached after the flower has bloomed white. The white blossoms will crinkle and lose their shape when they are dried, but the green dry well after a period of two weeks by hanging with their heads down.

22. An exotic arrangement whose center of interest
is a rosette made of desert spoons grouped around a
magnolia seed cone. The dried palm fronds and the
leaves of the *Ficus decor*, a plant similar to the rubber plant, are in harmony with the focal point.

If you have the variety of hydrangea listed as Paniculate, leave the
blooms on the bush until fall. By then its color has become bronze mixed
with a pale green near the base of the flower. It is very pretty in arrangements and dries well by hanging. Allow two to three weeks for it to dry.

Usually the bloom of either the Paniculate variety of hydrangea or
the Hills of Snow is too large to use in most arrangements. However, the
main stem branches into several smaller stems, each holding a cluster of
tiny flowers. The individual clusters can be broken off after the blossom
has dried, and then wired as you would a single flower.

You will want to dry an abundance of a delicate-looking plant called
artemisia, as it blends with many flowers and is especially good for outline

in your arrangement. Choose the variety called Silver King, whose tiny leaves are silvery white. Gather it with long stems, and do not defoliage, but hang the whole sprigs inverted to dry. Allow about two weeks for this process.

Salvia, another plant that is very useful, grows in shades of white, blue, and red. The last is better known as scarlet sage. All three varieties dry well by hanging and can be used in about two weeks.

DRYING CALYXES OF FLOWERS

The calyx of most flowers is the green bowl that holds the petals of the bloom. After the bloom has withered and fallen away, the calyx remains to support the seed-bearing organ of the plant. These, dried, are often very pretty and bring that elusive quality called "originality" to your design.

The gladiolus spike whose blooms have withered and fallen still retains the calyx of each blossom. Cut these spikes long and dry them by hanging, allowing about three weeks, as the stalk is heavy.

In the fall, be on the lookout for any shrub or tree that may retain the calyxes of the flowers. The shrub called Rose of Sharon is an example. Its dainty form is almost as pretty as the blossom. Poplar trees have nice tulip-shaped calyxes that appear in the fall and are dry when you pick them. Cut the branches as long as you will need them for your arrangements, but be careful not to damage the shapes of your shrubs or trees.

USE HERBS IN YOUR DRIED ARRANGEMENTS

Many herbs are as ornamental as they are useful, and flower arrangers as well as cooks will enjoy a small herb patch. Some herbs with pleasant, pungent odors, such as pennyroyal, are wild, inconspicuous plants which you weed out of your garden. Others will have to be grown in your garden as cultivated plants. For lovely foliage plants, mints, thymes, and artemisia, which has already been mentioned, are extremely useful. Choose half a dozen plants of the foliage herbs to start your herb garden, and your interest will be such that you will soon be adding more. Some say they have no space for herbs, but in every garden there is some spot just waiting for the right plant. Many will fit into your rock garden or make edgings for your vegetable garden or border a garden path. Usually it is best to buy the plants of most herbs rather than to try to sow seeds. The root of one mint plant will multiply until you wonder if it is going to take the whole garden. Most herbs prefer sun or at least part sun, and must have good drainage.

Herbs do not depend on their blossoms for beauty as do the other garden flowers. You may work and wait for weeks before your rose bush blooms, and unless it is dried, it is gone in a few days. But in the herb garden there is more lasting interest. Herbs can be very colorful, not only in their bloom, but in their leaves also. They will vary from the pale yellow-green and light gray to rich, dark greens. Their texture is interesting and ranges from the velvet-like mullein to the pebbly look of sage, rough-textured mint to the smooth artemisia.

The fragrances of a dried aromatic bouquet in your home will take you back to your childhood, when you sniffed the odor of an herb from your mother's garden. Oddly enough, the fragrance of the same herb will differ during the day, and is affected by rain and sun.

There will be some odors you will prefer to others, and the selection for your own herb garden will be a very personal one. Choose those plants which, when dried, will be refreshing and pleasing to you and your family.

Any dried bouquet will be a delight not only to the eye but to the nose if you tuck in a sprig of sweet-smelling lavender or mint. If it does not blend with your other dried flowers, it will not have to show. Wire the herb to a florist's pick and insert it at the back of the arrangement. Many herbs.have decorative value as well. The tiny blooms of lavender which our grandmothers dried and used in sachet bags do not lose their shape when dried. It should be picked at the height of its bloom, usually about mid-summer. The time of year may vary, however, with the locality and growing conditions. Cut it with a long stem, do not defoliage, and hang it inverted to dry for about two weeks.

Sage dries to a lovely gray-green color with an interesting pebbly texture. It retains its familiar odor when dried, as does thyme and wild mint. When processing herbs, hang them in small bunches, inverted, in a dark, warm area where there is good circulation of air. Never attempt to use them until they are entirely dry, as they will droop or mold in the arrangement. Allow two to three weeks for most herbs.

PODS, BURRS, NUTS, AND BERRIES

There are many interesting and attractive ways in which you can use pods. As most plants form seeds that are protected by some type of pod, many varieties are available. Some have a smooth exterior and may be filled with a "fluff." Others, such as burrs, are spiny on the outside. These are very effective in modern and large rough designs that might be suitable for your den, terrace, or playroom.

Gather pods at different stages of their development—that is, from their first appearance on the stalks, when the pods are small, tender, and a light green in color, until they are brown, dried, and often split open. You will then have a nice variety of colors and shapes to add to your collection. Cut the stem long and allow the pods to dry on the stalk. Tie several stalks together and hang, inverted, to dry. Allow three weeks for

23. This charming antique wooden wall bracket holds a gay array of sumac clusters, acorns, cones from an evergreen, the blossoms of the achillea, and a pomegranate, all silhouetted by the bronze beech leaves. This lovely color is the result of picking the beech in the autumn and processing it in a solution of glycerine.

most pods to dry, adding a week for those that are large, green, or especially moist.

Poppy pods, especially the annual variety, are smaller, daintier, and usually much prettier than the Oriental or perennial types. Cut them with long stems and allow two to three weeks for drying.

Lotus pods, although they are very large and may require three or four weeks to dry, are interesting and can be used with heavy material.

Okra pods picked at various stages of their development yield different colors. You may find many degrees of color gradation on the same stalk, the smaller pale green at the top, and big beige-colored pods toward the bottom of the plant. Different varieties of this plant also give a wide range of color. Dry the pods on the stalk by hanging for about two weeks. As the okra pod dries, it will split along its segments, giving the appearance of white stripes marking the length of the pod, a most unusual effect.

Milkweed is wild and seems to grow in most localities. You can get various sizes and colors by picking it at different stages in its development. Unlike many other pods, the milkweed pod has but one valve or segment. As it ripens on the stalk it opens, displaying a smooth seamless interior. A long, narrow organ called the placenta is attached to the base of the pod and bears the seeds. The green pods can be split, spread open, and the seeds removed. If the pod is braced in this position during the two-week drying period, the inside will assume a yellow color and the outside remain green. This combination is very effective. The milkweed pod will close if some means is not found to hold it open during the drying time. To accomplish this, insert segments of matchsticks or toothpicks to keep it from closing.

If you would like to simulate a calla lily, gather the green milkweed pods, removing the seeds very carefully from the placenta, which should be left attached to the base of the pod, as in Figure 3. This long, slender organ will now appear to be the stamen of your graceful calla lily.

The Chinese lantern, or Physalis, is one of the most beautiful pods, appearing in the second year after the seed of the plant is sown. The little pods, which look like bright red lanterns, dry nicely by hanging in ten days or two weeks, and last indefinitely. Ground cherries are similar in shape and dry equally well, but lack the brilliance in color of the Chinese lantern.

The pod of the unicorn, or Martynia, as the catalogues list it, has two odd-looking "horns" protruding from a rather large pod. It may provide just the interest you need in a modern arrangement. It dries easily by hanging in two to three weeks.

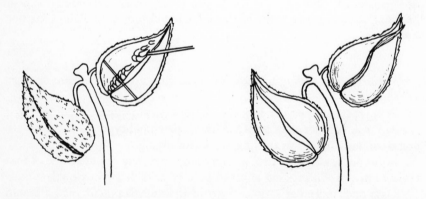

Figure 3. A green milkweed pod allowed to wither after it has been cut may be forced open and held during the drying process. For this, a segment of matchstick, toothpick, or small stick can be used. The sketch also shows how to remove the seeds from the placenta. The pod, with its smooth seamless interior, now resembles a calla lily.

Teasel pods were used by our grandmothers for combing wool, as their numerous spines were strong and sharp enough for this purpose. These should be used with rough material.

Love-in-a-mist ripens into a small lantern-shaped pod of five segments rather reddish in color. Cut it with as long a stem as possible and hang about two weeks to dry.

The seed-head of tithonia is not especially colorful, but its form is flower-like, and it will be attractive nestled in a dry bouquet. Allow about two weeks for it to dry.

Burrs of the castor bean, chinquapin, and chestnut will provide distinction in some designs. But the burrs should be picked while they are green and given at least three or four weeks to dry. If they are cut after they have opened, they are apt to drop from their stems. Burrs are most effective used with rough materials.

Nuts, also, such as those of the hickory tree, will stay on their stems if they are picked while they are green. Hazel nuts are especially pretty with their ruffly outer coverings. If these are picked at different stages of their development, they will range in shade from light green to a lovely rosy beige. Nuts will require several weeks to dry entirely, but they can be used as soon as they are picked because of their woody stems and tough exteriors.

Many berries, such as the bright-red nandina, will bring color to your arrangement. Nor should the dark-blue berry of the common bramble be excluded. Hang these with the berries down, and allow two to three weeks for them to dry. Bittersweet and pyracantha are especially decorative berries, even though they may shrivel a bit as they dry.

PLANT MATERIAL FROM THE WOODS AND ROADSIDE

You can add to your collection of dried materials by gathering beautiful plants that grow wild along the roadside or in the woods. Most of these dry by hanging heads down for a period of two to three weeks.

Sumac is well known in most parts of the country, as its many varieties are widely distributed. The large velvety seed clusters are usually more suitable with arrangements of rough-textured materials. They can be gathered from late summer into winter. Approach sumac with caution, however, as some people find it to be poisonous.

Goldenrod grows in profusion in most sections of the country. You will want to pick it at its peak of bloom when the flower head is rich yellow at the tip and just opening next to the main stem. If it is cut too early in the season it will be green in color; if left on the plant too long it will shatter and turn brown. Dry some of the many varieties of goldenrod for interest in form and color. You will want to use it with your delicate arrangements of roses and larkspur as well as the rough-textured types.

Joe-pye weed blooms in a large dome-like cluster of small lavender-colored florets. These should be gathered with long stems while they are still in the bud stage and dried by hanging with the flower head down. The whole cluster may be used in large compositions or a portion may be broken off to suit your needs.

Mullein is a weed whose tall, yellow stalks are seen blooming during the summer along the roadside and in fields. The *first growth* of this plant, found in the early spring and again in the fall, is useful to the arranger. When the young leaves sprout from the root system, they look like velvety petals of a pale-green flower. These rounded leaves, growing concentrically, form a rosette, which should be pulled from the ground by the roots and hung to dry. After most of the moisture is out and the leaves feel rather limp, place the mullein rosette in a box and arrange the leaves in the manner in which you want them to dry. Sometimes bits of shredded facial tissue placed between the leaves as they dry will support them in a more natural position.

Lady's-thumb is a paler pink than its cultivated cousin, lady's-finger, which has already been mentioned. You will find it growing wild along fences of the farmer's barn lot or in open fields. There may be instances when you prefer its delicate coloring and size to the cultivated species. Pick it when the tiny florets start to open along the bottom of the spike. Cut it with long stems, defoliate, and hang it as quickly as possible.

Grasses, mentioned before, are especially useful in most types of dried arrangements. The kinds that you gather will depend on where you live. Bring in as many varieties as you can find. Cut an abundance with long stems at different stages of their growth from the first tender green shoots to the tall spikes heavy with ripening seeds, as they are easily dried and stored.

An exotic-looking plant called "beechdrops" grows paracitically on the roots of the beech tree. Occasionally you will find this odd growth under beech trees springing six to twenty inches high from a thick scaly base. Hang these to dry for about three weeks. The unusual coloring and form will add distinction to your arrangement.

Pearly everlasting, or "rabbit tobacco," is excellent for a touch of silvery white to lighten your arrangement. White is often difficult to find. Pick it while it is in the bud and hang immediately to dry.

Magnolia (grandiflora) in some southern climates can be found growing wild in the woods and along the roadside. Boughs of this beautiful tree can be hung or merely laid in a box left open for free circulation of air. The leaves dry retaining a beautiful color and texture without further treatment. Also they can be processed by glycerine, described in the next section.

Roots and bare branches found in the woods and along the roadside will give distinction to your modern-line arrangements. Often the contour of the branch itself will suggest the design. It might seem that roots would be hard to find, but if you walk along a country lane where a road grader has cut into the bank, you may find exposed roots. In the case of rhododendron, which is on the conservation list of many states, removing an exposed weathered root could not damage the plant, and need not bother your conscience. Photographs 39, 40, and 41 show the construction of a line arrangement, illustrating the use of rhododendron roots.

Branches of shrubs and woody vines, such as wisteria, often suggest an interesting line. A few roots and branches may need to be cleaned, scoured, or in some cases sand-papered, but ordinarily those bleached by exposure to the elements are the most attractive. Some authors suggest coating roots and branches with solutions of shoe polish or wax, but we prefer the more natural weathered look. Usually no solution of stain, dye, or shiny substance is suggested in this book for any dried material—the exception being gilt or white enamel for special holiday arrangements.

FARM PRODUCTS

Most of the farm products dry best by hanging with the flowers or seed-heads down.

Wheat, oats, and millet are good for height and outline in your arrangement. Beardless wheat has a stronger stem and will remain upright, whereas the heads of the bearded variety tend to droop after they are

24. This unusual container has been made by peeling a segment of a log, leaving a smooth, delicately colored surface. The arrangement is of curved branches, grape leaves, ti leaves, and pods. Wood roses form the center of interest.

25. Miniature cattails and Oriental poppy pods give height to this arrangement. The warm colors of the strawflowers, bayberries, and magnolia leaves blend with the small ears of calico corn, an inviting spot of interest for a den or family room.

dry and may spoil the lines of your design. Oats are best used in clusters, several stalks together, as the ripened seeds are delicate and not strong enough to stand alone.

For interesting spikes and background, use the blades and husks of corn which will range in color from whitish-green through a golden-tan, streaked with burgundy. The foliage of Indian corn is especially colorful. Blades of corn should be pressed to dry. A description of this process is found in the next section.

Ears of corn are charming in Thanksgiving and harvest-time arrangements. Those of the Indian and calico, or rainbow, corn are smaller and more colorful. If the two varieties of corn are planted near one another in the garden, the colors will mix. In the fall when you husk the ears, each will be a delightful surprise package, for no two ears will be alike. To dry the corn, pull the husks back but do not remove them from the ear. Tie two or three of the husks with twine and hang the ear to dry; or simply spread the ears of corn with their husks pulled back on the floor or in an open box. If possible, put them in the sun to dry. Be sure both ear and husks are completely dry before you store them. Large baskets are especially good for storing corn, as they permit free circulation of air.

The ears of the strawberry popcorn are rosy-red, shaped like an oversized strawberry. Do not strip the husks from the pretty little ears, but spread them open and place them in an uncovered box. Be careful not to crowd them. After they are dry, the husks can be trimmed with scissors, each rounded like the petal of a flower. The rosy little ear of corn will be the center of the simulated blossom.

The tops of these varieties of corn picked while they are young and tender, before they have fully ripened, can frequently be used.

The ruby-red of pomegranates sparkles like a jewel in your winter bouquet. Buy these at the market and prick them in an inconspicuous place to allow them to dehydrate more quickly. They should be placed where the air can circulate freely, and stored in an open box to avoid becoming moldy.

Gourds, too, need the same treatment of a small puncture to facilitate drying. Some flower arrangers shellac or wax their gourds, giving a rather artificial look, but here again the natural surface of these garden products is more pleasing.

Photograph 26 shows a gourd used as a container. After it was dried, the opening for the flowers was cut with a sharp knife and the seeds removed. This gourd is several years old and still in good condition.

Lichens are flowerless plants that grow on bare rocks and tree stumps all over the world. They have neither roots, stems, nor leaves, but consist of irregularly shaped extensions called "thalli." You have seen patches on rocks that resemble tiny shells. These are crustaceous lichens, usually gray or gray-green in color. On the branches of old fruit trees you frequently find the scaly little lichen growth of brown and tan lobes. Break off these branches, preserving the interesting scale with its subtle coloring.

On your next walk through the woods, examine every tree stump and fence rail for the leaf-shaped lichen known as the "foliose" lichen. They are often highly colored, perhaps white beneath and green on top. Others are fan-shaped with orange, tan, and brown striations. Their texture is velvety, pleasing both to sight and touch. Collect all you can of these unusual plants and dry them in freely circulating air and store in an uncovered box. When they are hard, you can wire them by pushing the heavy florist's wire (No. 18) through the base. Group several together into a rosette, forming a focal point for an arrangement of dock, strawflowers, and pods. This would be charming in a pottery bowl or natural reed basket against a paneled wall.

Photograph 27 shows a design whose center of interest is a lichen rosette made by pushing the base of each lichen into the ball of clay. Gladiolus spikes and clusters of nuts complete the design.

26. Even a gourd can be utilized as a container by cutting an opening, scooping out the seeds and pulp, and allowing it to dry. A ball of clay placed inside the opening holds an arrangement of bittersweet tendrils, lichens, and straw-flowers.

Cattails, which grow in marshes in most sections of the country, furnish an interesting form for some types of designs. These should be cut before they reach maturity—that is, when they are green or beginning to show a tan color. The mature cattails, a deep brown in color, will burst and shatter after they are brought indoors.

If you live in Arizona you may be familiar with the miniature cattails. These are very useful in many types of arrangements. They can be purchased in some florists' shops if they are not native in your section. If you cut the common cattail while it is tiny, pencil-slim, and green, you will have a dainty miniature that will last for years. Cattails can either be hung or placed in a jar to dry.

Pussy willow, tame or wild, should be cut before it is too mature, when the little gray furry bundles first appear. If they are placed in water, they will bloom out and spoil the effect. Therefore, place them in a dry jar or hang them.

In those regions where vegetation is limited, you will have to put to use that which is available. For example, across the Mid-Western plains states the tumbleweed grows profusely, breaking from its stem when it is mature. It often travels many miles, bouncing over fences, carried by the wind. Nature has provided this means for scattering their seeds. But if you bring in a tumbleweed already dried by nature, you can pull the slender stems together, breaking off suitable sections to give "line" to your design. A design was fashioned in just this way using the tumbleweed for outline and filling in with rough material of neutral colors.

If the foliage described in this chapter does not grow in your section or if your foliage is scarce, experiment with what you have. The result may be much more original and pleasing.

27. A group of velvety-textured lichens placed in clay to form a rosette is the center of interest of this strikingly graceful design. Notice the cluster of hickory nuts blending their subtle coloring with the soft tones of the magnolia and gladiolus foliage. Three annual poppy pods complete the design.

28. Beware! That is a wasp's nest beside the pomegranate resting on the milk-crock lid. The container
is a large lichen reclining on an old cast-iron mortar.
The arrangement has been fashioned of Western
tumbleweed which was softened in water until it was
pliable. Cockscomb and evergreen cones create a
bright focal point.

V

Processing Foliage

Several arrangements in this book have been composed entirely of dried blossoms omitting leaves altogether, and the effect is pleasing. But most arrangements are complemented by the use of natural-looking foliage. Indeed, it is possible to use foliage alone—say, preserved magnolia leaves in a brass container or bronze beech leaves in a pottery bowl. The larger leaves can be used with pods, nuts, berries, or grains to create striking modern designs, or compositions that would be charming in a den or a recreation room. For these, dried blades of corn, rosettes of mullein, large magnolia leaves, or pressed autumn leaves are suitable. But to complement a very delicate grouping of, perhaps, roses, larkspur, cockscomb, hydrangea, and statice, glycerinized ivy leaves or pressed fern fronds with a spray of beech or rose leaves would be more appropriate.

When we consider that all trees, shrubs, vines, ground covers, and herbs bear leaves of varying shape, color, and texture, there is no limit to the use we can make of processed foliage.

Not all leaves can be processed, of course, just as some flowers cannot be dried. Those listed here will give you an idea of the type of leaf which will respond to some method of drying. Try the foliage of trees and shrubs native to your locality which may not be mentioned here. The plants named in this chapter are by no means all that can be preserved but are those that give the best results for most flower arrangers.

There are several ways of processing leaves. In Chapter III you may read of sand-drying a few leaves such as rose foliage, the leaves of sunflowers, and sprays of ivy. However, pressed leaves and those processed in a solution of glycerine and water are the most frequently used. Some books describe intricate ways of skeletonizing leaves, but the problem here is removing the leaf tissue, leaving only the leaf veins. The tissue must be either decomposed or eaten away by chemicals, and both are unpleasant methods with doubtful outcome. Skeletonized leaves can be bought at the florist if you have a need for one of these fragile forms in your arrangement.

FOLIAGE DRIED BY NATURE

In late fall, nature has dried artistic-looking leaves on the plant which can be picked ready for use in your arrangement. While you are out gathering pods and berries, be on the lookout for any leaf that has dried in an interesting form or unusual color. If it is stemless, you can add an artificial stem to a leaf by placing a No. 18 florist's wire parallel to the lower half of the central vein, allowing it to extend several inches from the bottom of the leaf. Then secure it in place with a length of Scotch tape.

AIR-DRYING

Many fresh leaves, such as slim forsythia foliage, can be dried by simply laying them on a flat surface and allowing them to dehydrate in the air—hardly a "process" at all. They may curl a bit as they dry, but they will have a more natural look than those that are pressed. Magnolia leaves dry in this manner, becoming a beautiful soft gray-green. If you want a flatter leaf, pick up those that have dropped to the ground under the tree and allow them to dry on a flat surface. These will remain flat, whereas leaves picked from the tree will curl. Try stacking your leaves one on top of another to dry. These will not curl as much and the color will be very natural. The small, narrow leaves of the forsythia dry well this way, as do the leaves of the nandina shrub and the buddleia, or butterfly bush.

The spike-shaped foliage of gladiolus is very useful in arranging. Cut the spikes long and place them on a flat surface to dry. They may curl a bit, but this will only add to their look of naturalness.

PRESERVING BY PRESSING

Probably the first method of drying plant material was by pressing. Our grandmothers placed a flower from a special bouquet between the pages of the family Bible for preservation. Pressing can give a very natural-looking appearance if the right steps are taken.

Some arrangers press blossoms as well as leaves, but pressing gives a flat appearance. Limit your plant material to be preserved by pressing to foliage. Blooms of all kinds retain their shape and color far better by either sand-drying or hanging, the method depending on the flowers. Charming designs for plaques, pictures, and shadow boxes can be made with dried flowers and foliage; the directions are given in Chapter VIII. Here the blossoms are not pressed but hung or sand-dried, and their depth gives a very natural appearance to the composition.

GATHERING FOLIAGE FOR PRESSING

Select foliage that is mature or well developed, but not old. The leaves are more apt to cling to the branch if you cut it while it is young. Also, foliage should be picked before there is danger of damage by insects or prolonged drought. Leaves that are to be successfully pressed must be really fresh. If any have withered since picking, try to revive them by putting them in water, but don't press them. When they are quite restored, they can be pressed.

In case the leaves are dusty, wash them, then remove all moisture from them. If necessary, prune the branches and trim away damaged leaves before arranging them for pressing.

The foliage of many flowers can be pressed to be added later to their blossoms to give a very natural look to your arrangement. When you bring roses in to dry, also cut some rose leaves to press. Place these carefully between the pages of a book, or, if you prefer, between layers of newsprint, seeing that no leaflets are folded or overlapping. Avoid too much pressure, as it will produce leaves that are too flat.

A branch of lilac foliage can be pressed, even though the stem is heavy, by placing it between folds of newsprint. If individual leaves drop away from the stem, do not destroy them. Each leaf can be wired by placing a length of heavy florist's wire along the central vein and securing the wire to the leaf by a strip of transparent gummed tape. Single leaves are frequently more useful than large sprays in arranging.

The butterfly bush has a slim, attractive leaf. The upper side of the leaf is dark green, while the under side is pale gray-green. Frequently the pale gray-green side of the leaf will blend more readily with your dried flowers than the darker side. With dried foliage, either side of the leaf can be used. These may be preserved by pressing the single leaves between the pages of a book.

Poppy foliage, the annual variety, has charm and an interesting texture for use with more delicate blossoms. These can be pressed between the pages of a book or of newsprint. Each little leaf will require an artificial wire stem Scotch-taped to the back after the leaves are dry.

The woods is an unlimited source of beautiful foliage suitable for pressing. When you walk through the countryside, take an old magazine and a large paper bag filled with folded newspapers. These will accommodate your larger branches, placed between the folds of paper, then into the paper bag. When you cut fern fronds and small leaves, place them between the pages of the magazine to keep them in good condition until you are ready to press them. If you are hiking, wait until the last possible moment to cut your leaves and branches to keep them as fresh as you can.

Many varieties of ferns growing in mossy clusters deep in the shadows of the woods will provide lovely lacy outlines for your dried arrangements. A very common one, which is suitable for pressing, is the Christmas fern (*Polystichum acrostichoides*). The fronds of this plant are mature in the fall and should be picked and pressed at that time. These can be arranged in the curve or line that you want them to assume as you place them between layers of newsprint. Weight them only enough to hold them in place.

Leaves of the wild beech are especially lovely in arrangements. Cut these while they are green, and also gather some later in the fall, when they have turned yellow, for a beautiful addition to your collection of pressed foliage.

Most of the colorful autumn leaves can be preserved by pressing. Gather them when they first become tinted, as they lose their color if left too long and are apt to drop from their stems after they are dried. The many varieties of maples are favorites because of their exquisite colors and delicacy of outline. Individual leaves or branches can be pressed. Remember never to discard a beautiful leaf that has fallen from the stem, as it can always be given an artificial wire stem and used in your arrangement. Most of the many kinds of oaks, especially those that are not too large, are useful in arranging. Dogwood, though conserved in some states, is lovely when pressed. Use it either green or after it has been frost-nipped. Sassafras, sourwood, gum, poplar, locust—in fact, most of the broad-leafed trees—can be processed by this method either green or after they have assumed their fall colors. This, however, excludes the conifers, which will shatter when dried by most methods.

HOW TO PRESS

Leaves and branches that are pressed under a definite pressure of weights, such as books, boards, or bricks, are very flat in form. Sometimes they are attractive in an arrangement, but those that are pressed between several layers of absorbent paper and weighted only enough to hold the paper in place are much more natural-looking. Find a flat surface that will not be used for at least two weeks, and place several thicknesses of newsprint over it. Place your leaves and branches, arranging them as you wish. If leaves overlap, slip folds of paper between them. Then, over all lay more newsprint and hold in position by boards, not heavy ones, or pieces of old carpeting—anything that will hold the paper in place. Permit them to lie undisturbed for at least two weeks. They can be tested for crispness by feeling the edge of a leaf, just as you test the petals of a rose being dried in sand. Occasionally foliage may require three or four weeks to be completely dry.

Some authors suggest changing the paper after the first twenty-four hours to improve the color of the leaves, but it is difficult to tell which leaf has had this additional treatment when a number are compared. If you bring in large branches and have no place to dry them, arrange them under the corner of your carpet or scatter rug, first putting down a layer of newspaper. You will be pleased at the natural look of your pressed flowers.

Your pressed leaves may remain in their newspaper folds for several months if you do not need the space. Also, to store them, you can place them in boxes, covering them carefully and labeling them.

Spike-shaped foliage is especially useful in arranging. Gladiolus dried in the air was mentioned at the beginning of this chapter. The spears can also be pressed between layers of newsprint, very lightly weighted, for a natural effect. Corn blades can be treated in the same way.

Scotch broom is a shrub whose boughs are used for outline in fresh arrangements as well as dried. These should be cut two to three feet long, defoliated, and curved in the line you want them to assume. This is done while they are green by winding a length of twine around a small bundle of the boughs and drawing the ends of the twine together, pulling the boughs into a semicircle. The ends of the twine are then tied together and the bundle laid on a flat surface to dry. This is not exactly a "pressing" method, but the resultant dark-green boughs are so rewarding to the arranger that they need to be mentioned. After ten days to two weeks, cut the twine away and store the boughs in a large covered box.

PRESERVING BY GLYCERINE

By far the longest-lasting foliage is that preserved in a solution of glycerine and water.

This is a preserving method, rather than drying, for the solution is carried through the plant's stem up into the veins and out into the tissues of the leaf. The vein structure of the leaf becomes more conspicuous as the glycerine penetrates the veins, giving them an "inked-in" look. Also a change in color can be observed as the solution progresses into the tissues, the color dependent on the kind of leaf. In general the fresh green leaf takes on a yellowish-bronze tone, giving colors ranging from light olive to a rich brown. Although they do not retain their original color, glycerine-processed leaves are extremely useful and attractive. An arrangement of this foliage by itself, that is, without blossoms, is beautiful.

The wild-beech leaf, distinguished by a paler green than most other fresh leaves, becomes a light olive after it takes the glycerine solution. If you cut the wild beech in the early fall, after it has turned yellow, and put it in a solution of glycerine, it becomes a beautiful bronze. Maple leaves cut when green take on the same light-olive color, the autumn-tinted leaves of maple becoming bronze.

The southern magnolia leaf, which is a darker green when fresh, be-

29. An antique pitcher of rich shades of brown was marred by a floral design painted on the front. This was turned to the back and a Hogarth curve was fashioned of Scotch broom, dried in a curve by the method described in this chapter. Glycerinized magnolia leaves are used as filler. The center of interest is a pomegranate whose color and texture blend perfectly with the foliage and container.

comes a rich velvety brown. Dainty galax leaves change to a golden bronze, while ivy and periwinkle deepen into olive green.

Although the leaf changes color when it takes the glycerine solution, it retains its flexibility and is pliable to the touch. When it is preserved by this method, it will last out of water for years. It can be wiped clean with a damp cloth and rearranged time after time.

Not all leaves will take the glycerine solution. Nor is it possible to give rules that will definitely guide you in selecting types of leaves to process with glycerine. But if you choose the leaves that have body, you will have more success. For example, the tougher leaves of trees seem to take the solution better than the tender leaves of annuals such as zinnias or marigolds. Woody vines like ivy and periwinkle do well in glycerine.

The age of the leaf is extremely important in the glycerine process—leaves too old or too young do not do well. On a sprig of ivy the young, tender terminal leaves may wither and not take the solution, while the middle leaves of the stalk process perfectly. Then, farther back on the stem, the older, tougher leaves may turn black or become spotted with black, thereby proving useless to the arranger.

If the trees and shrubs described here are not native to your section of the country, you will want to experiment on preserving leaves that may have similar characteristics. It is fascinating to try different kinds of leaves, observing them daily to see the changing colors. If the leaves are unable to take the solution they will wilt in a few days, and you can try others.

HOW TO USE GLYCERINE SOLUTION

Select leaves that are well developed, not too young and not too old. If you wait too late in the season, they may be damaged by insects or blight. Cut a branch of the leaves not more than two feet long. The farther the solution has to travel, the longer the leaves at the top have to wait for the preserving glycerine, and they may wilt before it can reach them. The best length is one foot to eighteen inches. This, again, depends on the kind of leaf in question.

If it is necessary to carry the leaves some distance—say, from a walk in the woods to your home—and there is danger that they may become wilted, you will want to place them in water to keep them fresh. But the sooner you put the branch in solution after it is cut, the better specimen you will have. Make sure your jars and solution are ready for the foliage as soon as it is cut.

The solution is made by mixing one part glycerine with two parts water. Some authors suggest equal volumes of water and glycerine, but such a rich mixture is not necessary. The glycerine is expensive, so, if possible, buy it in bulk for economy's sake. All drugstores carry it. Choose a container that has a small aperture, such as a quart milk bottle, in order to restrict evaporation. However, the solution evaporates at a slow rate, and this need not be a source of concern. The bottle needs to be large enough to provide stability for the larger branches. Fill your jar with the solution to a depth of four to six inches. This will be determined by the size of the branch you wish to process.

Wash the branches and leaves under a spigot of cold water and trim away any damaged leaves. With a bit of cotton soaked in the glycerine solution, wipe the surface of each leaf, as some moisture is absorbed through the leaves as well as through the stems. This will help to prevent wilting. If you notice wilting during the processing period, you can remove the branch long enough to wipe the leaves with a pad of cotton soaked in the solution.

Pound the stems of the branches until the bark is broken and the center well frayed, about two to three inches up on the stem. This is done in order that the stem may absorb the mixture more quickly. Some authors suggest peeling the stems or slicing them for an inch or two, but the hammer strokes seem to shred the woody stem end more effectively and more easily. Place the branches stem down in the solution, making sure that the liquid covers the crushed part of the stem. Process only a few branches at a time in order that sufficient glycerine will be available for each leaf (see Figure 4).

Leave them in a dry, well-ventilated room until total absorption has taken place. A damp, cool basement is not desirable for processing leaves, as they may mold. Perhaps you have a pretty container for the solution

Figure 4. To glycerinize leaves, pound the stems of the branch and place them in a solution of glycerine and water. See text for kinds of leaves, length of time for the process, and how to prepare the solution.

and you can enjoy the beauty of your leaves while they are processing in your living quarters. Watch them, being careful that the solution does not evaporate. Add more from time to time, keeping the level of the liquid above the crushed part of the stems.

After several days you may notice that a new color is spreading from the veins of the leaf outward. In the case of the magnolia, a rich dark-brown color can be seen, first outlining the skeleton of the leaf, then creeping into the leaf's tissues. The change in color will be gradual. You will notice more and more of the brown shade as you inspect the magnolia leaf each day. As soon as this new color has spread to the edge of the leaf, the latter will feel pliable to the touch. The branches should then be removed from the solution and stored in a box or on a shelf. When the leaves are left in the solution too long they take on an oily, dark look that is not desirable. Some authors advise leaving the leaves until the edges begin to "ooze," but this will give poor results.

The ground covers such as galax, ivy, and periwinkle absorb much of their moisture through the surface of the leaves and for this reason should be immersed in the solution. Use a large, shallow casserole—either metal or Pyrex: the material seems to have no effect on the solution— with a lid to prevent evaporation. Fill it half full of the glycerine solution and place the individual leaves well below the surface. They may need to be weighted with a small rock, for wherever a tip of a leaf emerges from the solution, it will not be processed and will spoil its appearance. Leaves may overlap and they may be placed one above another and will still take the solution. Just be sure that all are under the surface of the liquid. The cut end of the stem may or may not be in the solution. This seems to make no difference.

Many kinds of individual leaves can be cut from the branch and preserved in this way. The large-leafed ivy with its long stem can be processed immersed in the liquid. Also sprigs of small-leafed ivy, cut ten to twelve inches long, may be immersed in the glycerine solution. If you use an oval casserole or other shallow container, the sprig of ivy can be bent to fit the curve of the bowl, giving it a nice line. This can be done for the periwinkle also. A small spray of maple leaves will process nicely immersed in the solution. Any leaf that will take the glycerine by stem can be processed in this manner.

Galax leaves are popular with arrangers all over the country, perhaps due to their charming heart-shaped outlines and their waxy dark-green appearance. They grow only along the slopes of the Blue Ridge Mountains through Virginia and North Carolina, however. Unless you live in this region, you will have to purchase galax leaves from your florist.

The Alba poplar trees have charming little notched leaves, silvery on one side, dark green on the other. In the solution the silvery side becomes a silvery gray; the dark green even darker. Branches of this tree should be pounded and placed in the mixture, allowing about ten days for the process.

Wild dogwood and rhododendron are conserved in many states. If they are available to you, both preserve well in glycerine. Cut branches of these and pound the ends two or three inches up on the stem before placing in the solution. The dogwood becomes a deeper green in about two weeks, and the rhododendron takes on a lovely bronze color. If the leaves fall from the stem while they are processing or after, they still can be wired for later use.

For variety, try processing some of the autumn leaves as soon as they begin to change color in the fall. If you wait until the leaves become too old, they will not take the solution.

TIME FOR GLYCERINE PROCESSING

The time necessary for glycerine processing depends on the kind of leaf and its age. It may vary from four days for small galax leaves to two weeks for a branch of magnolia. It is well to note the date on which you start processing and check the leaves daily after the fourth day.

Part Two

ARRANGING
DRIED-PLANT MATERIAL

V I

Principles of Design

⚶ The modern homemaker needs to be proficient at many tasks, but those that are creative tend to make her routine less boring. The ability to make a pleasing arrangement of flowers either fresh or dried for her home, her husband's office, or to take to a friend, is just as necessary these days as the ability to make a taste-tempting dish from a group of culinary ingredients.

The emphasis in Part II will be on the actual construction of arrangements that will enhance the home as well as those that are meant for exhibiting in flower shows. In other words, beauty, charm, and appropriateness will be first in importance instead of strict adherence to the rules set by the flower-show committee. As in all creative activity, that which is pleasing to the individual is largely a matter of one's basic character, personality, and taste. Therefore each arrangement or composition is highly personal and its originality is an expression of the designer.

In this book, arrangements more closely resemble freshly cut bouquets rather than the amorphous masses of seed pods and pressed leaves we used to think of as "dried arrangements."

Charming compositions can be made with dried materials, using the ever-popular ceramic figures, the colorful and beautifully wrought figurines of birds, small animals, or children, unified on a bamboo mat or a wooden base. These may be much more interesting and decorative than a dozen purchased roses.

COMBINING FRESH AND DRIED MATERIALS

It is also possible to combine fresh flowers with dried materials in one arrangement. Possibly in winter a few red carnations could be used with glycerinized ivy leaves or gold chrysanthemums with bronze magnolia foliage. When you have a nicely shaped outline of dried materials, you can keep it and add fresh blossoms as a center of interest, replacing them as you need. In winter, you can arrange your lovely rosy strawflowers with fresh leaves from any house plant to make a bright centerpiece for your dinner table.

There are a number of ways to place fresh and dried materials in the same container. Remember, first, that the heavy woody stems of branches of magnolia or beech leaves will not be harmed if placed on a needle holder in water for a few weeks. If your arrangement is largely fresh, you can make your floral design on a needle holder in water, then place the branches of dried foliage on the holder just as if they were fresh. However, if your arrangement is predominantly dried, make it on a sand or clay base, treating it as though it were entirely dried, then place the stems of your fresh flowers in a small glass vial. A test tube or a small discarded Alka-Seltzer bottle with water in it is good. The little bottle can be anchored in the clay or thrust into the sand. For a few fresh flowers in a dried arrangement, use a child's deflated balloon, with water inside, and close it at the top around the flower stems with a rubber band or a wire. It can then be secured to a florist's pick and placed as you wish in an arrangement.

LET THE FLOWERS SUIT THE LOCATION

Of course you will want to grow and eventually dry those flowers whose colors are pleasing to your taste and harmonious with the color scheme of your home. You will also take into consideration the location in which you plan to display the flowers. Will it be against a wall? If so, viewed from only three sides? Or will it be on a table, "in the round," so to speak, and require careful design to be viewed from all sides? Will it be high to the eye's level, or will it be placed low? Many an arranger has been disappointed by making an arrangement on the kitchen table, then placing it on the mantel in the living room, only to see that at this angle it is not pleasing. It isn't always possible to make your arrangement on the spot where you expect to place it, but you can study the position and then design your flowers on about the level you expect to view it. Is the location in which you plan to display your flowers the focal point of the room? If so, you may want your design to be more dramatic and eye-catching than if the position is secondary and needs flowers that complement the area.

ESSENTIALS OF GOOD FLOWER-ARRANGING

As in any artistic endeavor, it is necessary to learn how to use the elements of the art in order to produce pleasing results. Many authors list components of arranging in various ways, but the essentials of flower-arranging, both fresh and dried, are *harmony, balance,* and *rhythm.*

Harmony will include color harmony, of course. To appreciate color harmony is natural to modern women who plan everything from their wardrobes, their interior decorative schemes, to the attractiveness of colorful foods and china on their dinner tables with the rules of color harmony in mind. When making an arrangement, be sure its colors are harmonious with its surroundings. The container must harmonize with the plant material, and the foliage and flowers themselves must be harmonious in color.

There must be harmony in texture as well. The texture of the container that will hold dainty flowers of fine texture, such as roses, larkspur, xeranthemums, and lady's-finger, should be also fine. It might be china or milk glass or silver, but never pottery or wood. For the latter a grouping of zinnias, daisies with pods, nuts, or berries would be appropriate. There must be harmony in the texture of the plant material itself. You would not think of mixing rough-textured pods or corn blades with roses, but they would do nicely with zinnias. Often you will be surprised to find that the textures of some wild growth of goldenrod, Queen Anne's lace, or joe-pye weed will be harmonious with fine-textured flowers. Many of the wild grasses can be used with delicate blossoms. The annual poppy pod lends itself to delicate arrangements, whereas the Oriental poppy does not.

Some authors would prevent the use of flowers that bloom in different seasons to be used together, but why dry flowers if not to use out of season? We have outgrown the ancient Oriental notions that we should not use Queen Anne's lace with forsythia, or blue hydrangea with dogwood, or pineapples with peaches because the first is tropical and the second is not! Now we feel that we can combine that which is truly harmonious in color and texture without regard for ancient dogma.

Second, there must be *balance* in any good arrangement. Balance is a satisfying distribution of color, shape, and weight. This brings us to the all-important matter of design. Every effective arrangement must have a well-thought-out plan of what it shall look like before it is started. Begin with the container. If it is low, shallow, or flat, it will probably call for a line or line-mass arrangement. A design that follows one principle contour is called a "line" arrangement. Thus a crescent or U shape follows the outline of a new moon; its points may be boughs of Scotch broom or tips of grasses (see Photograph 7, which is a crescent). Flowers and foliage are placed low to fill in. For this type a shallow bowl is excellent. An S shape, or Hogarth curve, as it is called after the painter, is a favorite line arrangement, and is shown in Photograph 5. A horizontal arrangement is just what the name implies; its principal line is low and horizontal, excellent for a dinner when the guests would like to be able to see one another across the table. The vertical arrangement is usually made in a deeper container and rises in a vertical line. Dried gladiolus leaves are good for establishing the line, as are tips of larkspur and lady's-finger.

The mass arrangement may appear to be a grouping of many more flowers, but it, too, has a plan. The outline of the mass may be oval, fan-shaped, or, more frequently, triangular. The line-mass is a combination of these two. Regardless of the outline or contour, the design must have balance. Let us imagine a vertical line or axis drawn through the center of the arrangement. There must be as much weight on one side of the arrangement as on the other. This is easily accomplished in a symmetrical arrangement in which both sides are designed to be mirrored images of each other. The fan shape and the isosceles triangle are examples of symmetrical design. It is more difficult to balance the asymmetrical design, in which the area of one side should be about the area of the other, even though one side may be shaped differently from the other.

"Weight," or "visual weight," as some authors call it, is also a matter of the size of the flower heads; the larger, of course, seeming to have more weight than the smaller. It is also a matter of color, the stronger colors seeming to present more weight to the viewer than the lighter colors.

For a feeling of stability, place large shapes low in your design and the smaller, lighter-colored flowers above them. Good composition requires that the design have a "center of interest" or a focal point, which usually is a flower form of intenser color and perhaps more fully bloomed out than the others. This, too, would be placed low and probably near the central axis.

A common fault among many beginning arrangers is to start the large plant material too high in the arrangement, giving a bushy, top-heavy look to the whole array. This is a matter of planning ahead and knowing just how you want the whole design to look. A pleasing practice among flower arrangers is to "break the line of the container." By this is meant that at some point a bit of plant material is brought over the edge of the container, breaking its line, to the eye. This is artistic, serving also to give balance to the design.

Finally, when you place the arrangement in the location for which you have designed it, see that there is balance in its surroundings. Is it too large or too small for the area on which it has been set? Is it in balance with the pictures or decorations on the wall behind it, and the accessories on the surface beside it? If it is asymmetrical, does it "point" in the right direction? All lines in good composition should lead the eye into the room or toward the center of the grouping, rather than toward a wall corner.

The third element or essential of a good flower arrangement, either dried or fresh, is that nebulous quality called "rhythm." Rhythm in an artistic composition gives a feeling of motion, that which keeps it from looking static or dead. Rhythm is achieved by a graceful grouping of forms and colors. The eye is compelled from one point to another by a pleasing gradation of size in the flower forms or shadings of color which define a definite line or pattern within the design.

In the following chapters you will be shown by pictures and step-by-step descriptions just how to put together three mass arrangements in deep containers, then how to prepare and arrange flowers in shallow containers. Two line arrangements are described, one in a deep container, the other in a shallow, followed by directions for arranging on a flat container. Two miniature arrangements are described, one on a poppy pod, the other an acorn cup. In addition to making arrangements, you will learn how to lengthen stems, group flowers, simulate a calla lily, a cornhusk flower, and a bud. Directions are given for making containers from bedposts, peeled logs, and gourds, and camouflaging tin cans with twine, felt, and paint for very attractive "pillow" vases. You will be shown exactly how to decorate a mirror and brush back for a little girl's room, and how to make shadow boxes and pictures with dried flowers, as well as costume jewelry and other novelties. Finally, you will be told how to care for your dried compositions and also how to transport them when you are eager to "show them off" to others.

VII

How to Make a Dried Arrangement

The reward for your time spent in drying beautiful plant material comes when you start arranging it in attractive and lasting designs. You are now an artist painting pictures with flowers, selecting colors and arranging their forms in the most pleasing combinations.

For ease and convenience while you work, plan ahead to have a well-lighted work space, equipped with a comfortable chair and table. Some kind of background is helpful in making either a fresh or dried arrangement. If your table has been placed against a wall whose surface is a pleasing neutral color, the wall may serve as background. Better yet, a large tinted cardboard background about twenty-eight inches high and fifty inches wide may be set up by bending about ten inches of each end of a piece of cardboard at right angles to form a "niche." Such niches are used at many flower shows to exhibit arrangements and are tinted in a pale shade of neutral or in harmonizing colors.

If the day you choose to make your arrangement is damp or rainy, the moisture in the atmosphere will make your flowers less brittle and easier to work with. Here the "light touch" is to be encouraged in handling dried flowers, as they are easily broken.

MATERIALS NEEDED IN MAKING
A DRIED ARRANGEMENT

In addition to your collection of beautifully dried flowers, you will need a sturdy pair of clippers and three weights of florist's wire: No. 18, No. 22, and No. 26. The first is heavy wire to be used for reinforcing stems; No. 22 is a medium size, used for grouping stems and wires together; the last, No. 26, is a very fine wire and will be used occasionally for tying. Green "florist's tape," purchased at the florist's, and "twist stems," small chenille-covered wires, are sometimes used. Of course you will want sand and clay for holding the stems of the plant material. The florist sells a new plastic clay that will adhere to the container, but modeling clay such as the children buy from the ten-cent store is also fine for this. However, if it is colored green or gray it is easier to conceal in your arrangement. It is also possible to use styrofoam, which you can buy at the florist's, and many flower arrangers do. If you are using a flat or shallow container, you will have to bind the styrofoam to the surface with melted paraffin. After the paraffin has cooled, it will harden and hold the styrofoam in place. In a deep container the styrofoam must be cut to fit and wedged tightly against the sides. Any design, fresh or dried, must be made on a solid foundation to be stable and satisfactory.

Another disadvantage of styrofoam is its toughness. To push a brittle stem into it would result in breaking the stem. Most stems other than those that are woody must be wired to a florist's pick before they can be placed in the styrofoam. Also, wherever a hole has been made in the styrofoam, it is there to stay. In clay the hole can easily be closed. In most instances clay is the more convenient to use.

And, of course, you will need a container that will harmonize with your dried-plant material.

CONTAINERS

One of the many advantages of working with dried flowers is the complete freedom you have in selecting your container. As no water is used, your container need not "contain" anything. Its requirements are so meager—just enough surface to hold a small mound of clay, its size depending on the weight of the dried material to be used in the arrangement. Any object that has possibilities of beauty or interest, from a flat piece of pine board to a silver epergne, may be used. Do not overlook your china cabinet as a source of containers. Nicely shaped sugar bowls, cream pitchers, bread trays, and soup tureens make very attractive containers.

Perhaps an old ironstone dish is now out of use because of a chipped edge or unsightly crack. Save it, as it will probably be lovely holding a colorful array which can be placed to conceal any defects.

If you have a nicely shaped vase whose color or decoration is not harmonious, you can camouflage it to look charming and utterly different by painting it.

Such a container is shown in Photographs 30 to 34, in which a mass arrangement has been made. It was painted a shade called Sheffield gray, which blends with most dried materials.

When using a deep container of this type, fill it with sand to within a half inch of the top. This gives weight and stability as well as providing a means of holding the stems of your flowers. If your container is transparent or translucent, so that the sand can be seen, use salt or sugar instead.

Knead a large piece of clay between your hands until it is soft and pliable and shape it into a fat biscuit whose diameter is the same as that of the top of the container. Place the clay on the container, firming it around the edge with your finger tips. If you want to use your clay again, place a piece of wax paper over the sand before the clay is added.

You may plan to have a group of flowers to curve out and down at one side of your arrangement as in Photograph 21. In this case, concentrate more clay at that point and pull it over the edge to accommodate this material. After the flowers have been placed, none of the clay will be visible.

CONSTRUCTION OF A MASS ARRANGEMENT IN A DEEP CONTAINER

Here are directions for making a mass arrangement in a deep container. Photographs 30 to 34 will help you to follow this method.

All the material used by the authors in making this design is over a year old, showing how well correctly dried flowers will keep.

Select the plant material you will want to use for the outline, or periphery, of the design. Tapering tips of feather grass have been used here, although some other types of grass or artemisia or larkspur could have been used just as effectively. The color of the grass blends well with the soft gray color of the container.

The outline pattern of this design is roughly a triangle, but many other types of arrangements are equally suited to this container. It is very essential in arranging either dried or fresh flowers to have a mental picture of the general design before you start.

Choose one spike to establish your "line of height," or the highest point of your design. Usually this height is one and one half to two times the height of the container. As this arrangement is being made to place against a wall, it will be viewed principally from the front and sides, rather than from all around, as for a table. Therefore, the tallest spike of grass has been placed well back on the exposed surface of the ball of clay to allow room for filling material (see Photograph 31).

Complete your outline, using the same plant material that you started with, then study it carefully from every angle. Stand away from it a bit or leave it for a time to get a new perspective—a good practice for any artistic endeavor. This is a particularly crucial point, as you want your outline to be correct and pleasing. It is almost impossible to change it after you have filled in with other dried material. When you are completely satisfied with your work so far, you are ready for the next step.

The periphery of the design is now filled in with some material that will give a lacy edge to the outline—in this case, dainty tips of pale-blue larkspur (see Photograph 32). By now the back of the exposed surface of clay is being rapidly filled with slim, brittle stems. If you use a florist's pick to adjust the stems in the clay or to tighten the clay around the stem, you will be less likely to break or damage your flowers.

30. Fill the container with sand to within a half inch of the top. Cover the opening of the container with a mound of clay and press it firmly in place. 31. Establish the outline of your design with skeleton material. 32. Fill in the outline with lightweight material—that is, plant forms of light color and small size. 33. Work in heavier material of larger size and darker colors, forming a smooth transition between the feathery edge and the focal point. 34. The finished product.

30

31

32

33

34

LENGTHENING SHORT STEMS

Unlike fresh flowers, if you have a dried flower whose stem is not long enough, it can easily be lengthened by one of three methods. As you work with your dried material, snipping the stems to the correct length, save these pieces of dried grass or flower stems. Save hollow stems especially, as they may be used later to lengthen those that are too short.

Figure 5a shows a stem that needs to be made longer but that is hollow, or soft-centered. You can push a florist's wire into this dried stem, cutting the wire the length you need to place the flower head at the right spot in your arrangement.

As is illustrated in Figure 5b, if the stem you wish to lengthen is sturdy enough, it can be pushed into a larger hollow piece of dry stem. Then cut the latter to the length you need for your arrangement.

As shown in Figure 5c, sometimes neither of these methods will work due to the delicacy of the plant. You can lengthen it, and at the same time reinforce it, by using either a discarded stem or a florist's wire in this way: place the piece of stem or wire parallel to the one you wish to lengthen, allowing the two ends to overlap an inch or more, depending on the weight of the flower head. Hold these two firmly in your left hand between your thumb and finger. Take a piece of the lightweight florist's wire (No. 22) in your right hand and place one end of it parallel to the overlap. Make a few turns around the upper portion of the wire and flower stem, then bring it down the length of the overlap and give it a few more turns, securing the lower portion. You can then clip the wire or stem to the length you need to place the flower in your arrangement.

The "joint" made by lengthening stems in each of these methods is concealed by the addition of other flowers, as is seen in the illustrations.

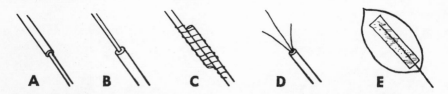

Figure 5a. A soft or hollow stem can be lengthened by inserting a florist's wire. Figure 5b. To lengthen a sturdy stem, push it into a larger hollow stem. Figure 5c shows another method for lengthening stems at the same time strengthening them. Place another stem parallel and overlapping an inch or so, then wind lightweight florist's wire around the two. Figure 5d shows several wire stems of flowers grouped together by thrusting them into a larger hollow or soft-centered stem. In Figure 5e a leaf without a stem need not be discarded. You can add an artificial wire stem by placing a length of Scotch tape to the back of the leaf.

Usually the only stems visible are the natural stems of the grasses and tapering tips of larkspur and the smaller flower or buds that show in the outline. If there is a possibility of a flower whose artificial stem may show, it can be covered by pushing it into a hollow, dried grass stem for a more natural look.

You may find a flower whose stem curves the wrong way. By cutting out the curve and adding a wire stem, you can bend it any way you wish.

FILLING IN THE OUTLINE

Now you are ready to fill in your outline. Starting from the outside of the design, work inward, adding filling material. If the flowers are placed somewhat symmetrically—that is, added to either side and top alternately—you are more apt to keep the arrangement in balance. The center of interest, sometimes called "focal point," is added last.

To fill this arrangement, pink larkspur and small strawflowers have been used, their delicate colors blending nicely with the blue larkspur and the gray of the feather grass.

When groups of flowers are wired together as a unit, such as the strawflowers seen in Photograph 33, they will stay just the way you place them without the annoyance of flower heads turning or springing out of position.

WIRING GROUPS OF FLOWERS

Arrange the flowers you want grouped together while holding them gently in your left hand. If the stems are not all long enough, and this is usually the case, you will need to lengthen them the same way you would lengthen a single stem. Place the heavy florist's wire (No. 18) parallel to the stems you wish to group, allowing an inch or two overlap. As you did with the single flower, wind a few turns of the lightweight wire at the top of the overlap and again at the bottom, securing the stems to the heavy wire. The latter can then be clipped to the desired length. Some dried flowers present a more pleasing appearance when grouped compactly rather than when allowed to stand separately.

The wire stems of strawflowers can be fastened together and at the same time lengthened, in the manner just described. Or, as in Figure 5d, several wire stems can be thrust into a soft-centered dried stem, which will hold the flowers in place. The stem of the celosia, or iris, is especially useful.

COLOR AND DESIGN WITHIN THE ARRANGEMENT

As you fill in the arrangement, you will want to study the color grouping and design within the arrangement itself. In general you will not adhere as closely to the rules of grouping colors when you are working with dried flowers as you would with fresh flowers. However, you do not want a splotchy look. This can often be avoided by using lighter shades of a color at the top of the arrangement, then adding deeper shades of the same color as you work toward the center of interest. Usually the center of interest is about the strongest color in the arrangement. A bit of white will frequently bring your dried arrangement to life.

Watch also that you have *an even distribution of shapes*—not too many points in one place or too many rounds. You will soon see that a large collection of dried material to choose from is a great help to the arranger. Then you will have just the right shape and shade of flower that you need. The round shapes are provided by flowers such as zinnias, achilleas, daisies, and strawflowers. The larger rounds should be placed low in the arrangement, and the smaller round forms higher. The long, pointed shapes, sometimes called "spike shapes," are the grasses, larkspur, gladiolus spikes, and others. Although these will usually be placed around the periphery of the design, some distributed throughout give depth to the arrangement.

Statice is neither round nor pointed, and is very useful as a transition between the two shapes.

The addition of foliage, either pressed or glycerinized, will provide variety of shape and color as well as give a feeling of naturalness to the arrangement. A rose flanked by pressed rose leaves is charming. A lacy fern frond or spray of beech leaves will complete your arrangement. Reserve heavier leaves such as magnolia to use with larger material.

ADDING THE CENTER OF INTEREST

There will be a transition between your filling material, already in place, and the *center of interest*. Usually this latter group of flowers is larger in shape and perhaps brighter in color. Sometimes a sharp demarcation will exist between the two groups. This too often spoils many fresh arrangements as well as dried. Be careful to add flowers of larger size and darker colors gradually to avoid this common fault (see Figure 6).

If you are planning to use very delicate flowers for your center of interest, these may be damaged by handling during your experimentation. Try a few sturdy strawflowers experimentally, placing them temporarily in the center to give you a chance to stand back and study the total effect of your work. Again, watch that your arrangement has depth by viewing it from all sides. If it is too flat, the addition of spike shapes will adjust this fault.

After you have decided on just what you want in the center of interest and where you want it—perhaps it is a cluster of roses grouped with pressed rose leaves—you can remove your temporary focal point and add these without fear of damage.

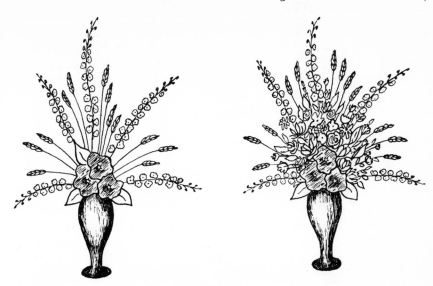

Figure 6. If there is a definite transition between your outline material and the center of interest, as in the picture on the left, you will need to add flowers of graduating size and color to fill this awkward gap.

The rule generally followed by most arrangers of fresh flowers is to allow some flower or leaf to cover a portion of the edge of the container. This is called "breaking the line of the container" and is a rule that holds also for the arranger of dried flowers. In this mass arrangement the entire ball of clay is hidden by filling materials placed with their short stems deep into the clay, also concealing a part of the edge of the container.

If your arrangement has been designed to be viewed from the front as this one has, there will be stems and wires visible at the back. To give the arrangement a more finished look, you may want to fill the back with leftover hydrangea, pearly everlasting, or a bit of damaged material.

OTHER TYPES OF DEEP CONTAINERS

Another deep container is the beautiful antique vase shown in Photograph 35. It, too, was filled with sand to a half inch from the top. Due to the wide mouth of the container, only a roll of clay has been placed around the top. This is done by softening a large piece of clay between your hands and rolling it until it is about one-half inch in diameter. Press the roll firmly around the edge of the container.

This mass arrangement was made following the method just described. The outline was established using grasses and lady's-finger. Notice the tiny poppy pods, statice, and the silky little xeranthemum, which give it a light,

35. This elegant array of roses, daisies, strawflowers, hydrangea, cockscomb, statice, lady's-finger, and xeranthemum complements the beautiful antique vase which holds it. Tips of dried grasses and tiny poppy pods add to its delicacy.

airy look. Roses, daisies, strawflowers, and cockscomb have been placed lower to create a center of interest. Larkspur, statice, and hydrangea were used as fillers.

Another deep container is shown in Photograph 36, which was made from a cylindrical tin can. After the surface had been coated with glue, fodder twine was wound, row close upon row, giving a delightful rough texture and a lovely gold color. It was filled with sand and topped with a ball of clay.

The arrangement in this container, although a mass type, is somewhat rougher than the masses previously described. The three tall pieces of gladiolus foliage were placed first, establishing the highest point of the design. The outline was completed by the pressed maple leaves, berries, and the three milkweed pods. Sea oats and bayberries were added for filler. The gold disks of the achillea fill the center of interest.

Instead of fodder twine, a jar or tin can may be covered with felt cut to fit the container. Again glue should be spread evenly over the sides and

36. The lovely gold color and interesting texture of this unusual container have been achieved by winding "fodder" twine on a cylindrical tin can. The gold color is repeated in the achillea, sea oats, and the interior of the milkweed pods. The design of the arrangement has been established by the tall gladiolus foliage, the bayberries, and the pressed maple leaves.

the cloth covering pressed on. Velvet could be used instead of felt. In this case the arrangement should be of more delicate flowers.

An attractive vase, nice for more modern arrangements, can be made from a liquid-wax can whose base is oblong rather than round. It could be painted or wrapped with twine, but is especially suited to a cloth covering. A container of this shape is sometimes called a "pillow" vase.

Photograph 38 is made of glycerinized beech foliage and galax leaves. The outline was completed with dried rose of Sharon seed pods and centered with chestnut burs, partly open and showing their ripe-brown chestnuts. The container was painted to harmonize with the subtle coloring of the glycerinized material. First a base coat of green was applied, then daubed while still wet with shades of yellow, orange, and brown. By using ten-cent-store glass vases of a good height and outline, you can have a supply of containers on hand, these to be painted with any combination of colors that will blend with your plant material.

In Photograph 29 an antique pitcher of rich shades of brown was marred by a floral design on the front. This was turned to the back, and a Hogarth curve fashioned of Scotch broom, dried by the method described in Chapter V. The center of interest is a pomegranate whose color and texture blend perfectly with the glycerinized magnolia leaves and the container.

USE OF BASES UNDER CONTAINERS

Bases placed under a tall container, perhaps an urn or a compote, are often the making of the arrangement, giving it balance and a look of importance. If accessories such as figurines are used to complete the arrangement, a base will serve to unify the grouping. Have several bases made of different woods and finishes, sizes and shapes. The base alone can be used as a container with just a mound of clay to support your material, as will be described under FLAT CONTAINERS.

SHALLOW CONTAINERS

For the shallow container, the one that is neither deep nor entirely flat, only a ball of clay is used to hold the arrangement. Make sure that the surface of the container is thoroughly dry. Soften a large piece of clay between your hands and form it into a ball. The size of the ball of clay will be determined by the amount of dried material it is to hold. Press the clay firmly against the bottom of the container.

Rice bowls make charming containers. The one seen in Photograph 37 with its airy bouquet, would enhance any home. It would look lovely on a coffee table or low end table, as it has been designed to be viewed from all sides.

The highest point in this arrangement is established first by placing a piece of larkspur or grass in the center of the ball of clay. Then, looking

37. Rice bowls make lovely containers for flowers of delicate colors and texture. This dainty bouquet is made up of larkspur, globe amaranth, statice, strawflowers, xeranthemum, and hydrangea.

down on the rice bowl, space larkspur or tips of grass around the center, not in an exact circle, but staggered artistically. View your design from all sides to be sure that it has balance and symmetry. Next add material, such as statice or feathery tips of cockscomb, to curve gracefully over the edge. Space them irregularly all around the lip of the container. Fill in with dainty flowers such as daisies, small strawflowers, xeranthemums, acroclinium, forget-me-nots, or bits of hydrangea. Artemisia and fine grasses will give it an airy look. Space and distribute your colors so that the arrangement will present somewhat the same appearance from all sides. Cut some pieces short and some tall to give high and low points for depth. This will prevent the arrangement from looking too spherical. As you add material, look down on it and view it from all sides for balance. This casual way of arranging gives the effect of a bouquet of freshly cut flowers.

Compotes, usually made of clear glass, milk glass, china, or metal, also require only a ball of clay to hold their arrangements. In the case of the clear-glass container you may want to paint it to conceal unsightly stems.

38. Chestnuts, rich and brown in color, are peeping from their bristly burs, surrounded by glycerinized galax and beech leaves. The outline consists of dried rose of Sharon seed pods, picked while still green. The container was one of the glass varieties that come from the ten-cent store and has been daubed with paint of colors that blend with the glycerinized leaves.

Many styles of arrangements are suitable for compotes. The dainty bouquet "in the round," just described, could be used; or a small version of the mass whose outline may be triangular or fan-shaped, as described in the first part of this chapter.

A modern *line arrangement* has been constructed in a metal compote shown in Photograph 41. The principles that apply to the construction of a line arrangement are the same for both fresh and dried flowers. First, *keep it simple*. In contrast to a mass arrangement, each branch should establish or help to establish a distinct line. Also, in contrast to a mass arrangement, no filler is used. A rule that applies to all arranging is especially true here: have a definite mental picture of the finished product before you begin.

If you have a collection of interesting and gracefully turned twigs, branches, and roots, you are off to a good start on a line arrangement. Rhododendron roots are especially graceful. However, if this shrub does not thrive in your section, there may be others just as effective.

Photographs 39 to 41 show how this type of arrangement is made. A ball of clay has been pressed firmly into the center of the container. As roots and pods have more weight than the flowers used in the mass arrangement, enough clay must be used to hold these firmly in place. Two rhododendron roots are used emerging from one point to give the effect of a single smoothly flowing line. These have been placed well back on the clay (see Photograph 39). As they establish your basic line, study them carefully for correctness of height and design. A pleasing height is at least one and one half to two times the height of the container. In the case of a flat container, the height is about the sum of the length and width of the container.

Photograph 40 shows the addition of three dried magnolia leaves. Their soft gray-green color blends well with the gray of the roots and the dull finish of the metal compote.

Finally, three lotus pods graduated in size are added to complete the picture, as is shown in Photograph 41. The largest pod was placed face forward in the center of interest, the second largest higher and turned slightly, while the smallest of the three is highest in the arrangement and seen in profile. The practice of placing some flower heads or pods to be seen in profile is always good and gives interest to your arrangement.

Another modern line arrangement has been constructed in a deep container as is shown in Photograph 1. This container has been painted, or rather dabbed, with a pastry brush in shades of gray, brown, light green, and dark green, each put on separately to give a marbleized effect, picking up the colors in the foliage. The container was then filled with sand to within a half inch of the lip, then topped with a ball of clay. Two ti leaves —grown in Hawaii and purchased from the florist's, then dried by the authors—were placed at the back of the clay. The taller of the two is about two times the height of the container. Another ti leaf has been thrust up

39. (*Left*) This is the first step in making a modern line arrangement in a brushed-copper compote. Only a ball of clay is used to hold the two rhododendron roots which emerge from one point to establish a smoothly flowing line.

40. (*Right*) In the second step the lines of the design are filled in by three magnolia leaves. Note that these have been placed to display the velvety texture of the underside of the leaves.

into the clay so that it points down. Next come two magnolia seed cones, one upright and the other placed with the seed cone down, following the line established by the ti leaves. Glycerinized magnolia leaves were added to complete the design, and a rosy pomegranate fills the center of interest.

To keep the pomegranate in place, use a florist's pick, the sharp end thrust into the soft stem end of the fruit. The other end of the pick can then be pushed firmly into the clay. This method is also used to secure ears of corn in an arrangement. The sharp end of the pick can be thrust

41. In step three the design is completed by the addition of three lotus pods, graduated in size. The lowest pod is seen face-on, the middle pod at an angle, while the highest pod is in profile.

into the soft pithy end of the ear where it has been cut from the stalk. The florist's pick is useful for many heavy materials, such as large pods, seed heads, and fruit.

URN-LIKE CONTAINERS

Urn-like containers are adaptable to dried arrangements, as the only preparation necessary is a ball of clay placed firmly in the container where you want to construct your design.

Such a container is seen in Photograph 42. It holds a modern line arrangement of blossoms made from cornhusks, dried magnolia leaves, and miniature cattails. As was just described in the first modern arrange-

42. These blossoms have been made of cornhusks trimmed to resemble petals. Several petals were then wired to an achillea which became the center of the flower. Dried magnolia leaves and miniature cattails establish the line of the arrangement. See text for instructions for making cornhusk flowers.

ment, the miniature cattails were placed well back on the ball of clay to establish the line of the design. The magnolia leaves came next, finally the cornhusk bud and blooms.

To make these unusual blossoms, trim the tops of a number of dried cornhusks with scissors in the shape of flower petals (see Figure 7). Gather in the fullness across the bottom and tie the gathers with a fine wire about an inch from the bottom of each husk. This leaves a short husk stem. Mold the petal with your finger tips, cupping it like a magnolia petal. For the center of the flower a marigold or houseleek or something similar could be used. In this case an achillea was chosen, its gold color blending with the yellow of the cornhusks. It is usually best to reinforce the stem of the central flower with a heavy florist's wire. Then, holding the stem and wire in the left hand, group the cornhusk petals around the stem with the right, and tie them all securely with a fine wire. Green florist's tape can be wound around the base of the petals and down the portion of the wire stem which might be visible.

The bud was fashioned in the same way, cutting cornhusks into small petals and holding them close around the wire stem without a flower center. The petals are wired to the stem and green tape wound about the base of the petals to form the calyx of the bud. If the wire stem of the bud

Figure 7. To make a cornhusk flower, trim the cornhusk along the dotted line to resemble a petal. Next, gather in the fullness across the bottom and tie the gathers with a fine wire. Finally group several of these petals around an achillea and secure them with green florist's tape.

will show, continue winding the green tape for several inches to give the effect of a natural stem.

For your fresh arrangements, try making cornhusk flowers of fresh husks, adding fresh marigolds or houseleeks. The greenish-white of the cornhusks is very unusual-looking.

FLAT CONTAINERS

Bread trays or small serving trays make nice flat containers (see Photo 7). Here again only a ball of clay is required to hold the arrangement. Wooden bases that are frequently used under taller containers can be used alone with just a ball of clay to hold an arrangement.

The container in Photograph 17 is an antique crock oven dish, the kind our grandmothers used for baking pies and cobblers. It has a gleaming, dark-brown interior, while the outside is a mellow, rather dull, tan color. Shallow in form, it needs only a ball of clay to hold the plant material. Dock, almost ripe, of a light-brown color outlines the triangular design. It is filled in with rich brown leaves of glycerinized magnolia cones and gladiolus seed pods. Cockscomb of a yellowish-tan color and pods of a greenish-tan complete the design.

UNUSUAL CONTAINERS

Driftwood, with its weathered gray and tan color tones, blends well with many types of dried materials. If the seashore or river bank fails to yield a suitable piece, try the woods, where you may find a knot of pine or oak. Occasionally a small tree stump or log bleached by wind and rain will make an attractive container. Florists' shops and novelty stores now carry driftwood and bleached branches for your use, also.

If you have found your driftwood out of doors, you may want to clean it with a stiff brush or sand any rough spots that might mar your furniture. Usually driftwood is washed clean by the elements and needs little in the way of cleaning or polishing.

As you study your piece of driftwood, consider its basic lines, which will, after all, dictate the design of the arrangement to be placed in it. Occasionally it is necessary to saw the driftwood to provide a base on which it will rest and serve to maintain it in its best position. A piece of felt on the bottom will protect your furniture.

Driftwood could be anchored to a base with clay placed at the back out of sight. With the clay you can raise and change the angle of your driftwood if it is necessary.

Next comes the arrangement. Here again it is especially important that you picture in your mind how the finished arrangement will look. In general, rougher textured materials are more suitable to driftwood. Materials from the field, woods, and roadside, such as dock, mullein, pods, nuts, and berries, would all be harmonious with driftwood. Some garden flowers of glowing colors, like zinnias and achillea, are complemented by the gray wood.

In Photograph 43, nuts of the buckeye tree have been picked while they were green to insure the nuts' staying inside the hull. These blend nicely with the rhododendron roots. The line of the design follows the curve of the driftwood. To hold the dried material, a ball of clay was placed toward the back so that it would be hidden by the container and its arrangement. A thin slate base gives importance and balance to the design.

An attractive container for rough materials can be made of a birch or oak bough, or of any tree whose bark is fairly smooth. Select a branch whose diameter is from three to six inches, and have a length of it cut to measure seven or eight inches. With the segment standing on one cut end, chisel a hole out of the other end deep enough to hold a ball of clay and the stem of the plants. An arrangement of rough, woodsy material in this container would be distinctive in a den or a recreation room. Also, you can peel the bark from the log segment, leaving a smooth, delicately colored surface on your container.

Photograph 44 shows a container made from a portion of a bedpost which was sawed from an old bedstead. It stands on one cut end; the other is now the top of the container. A hole was dug into the top end large enough to hold a mound of clay. In this there is a line arrangement, the design established by honey-locust pods. The center of interest is cockscomb and processed galax leaves.

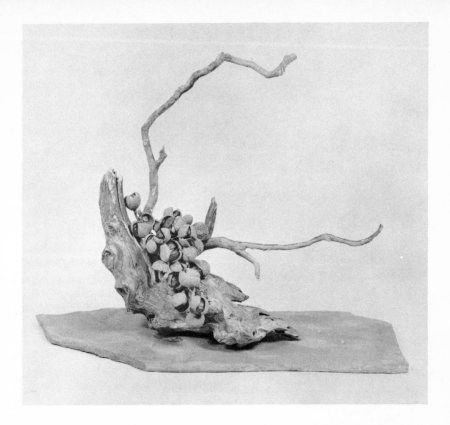

43. A graceful piece of driftwood on a thin slate base is enhanced by rhododendron roots and a cluster of nuts of the buckeye tree. These are held in place with a ball of clay.

Many kinds of *sea shells* can be used with dried materials. A ball of clay tucked inside will support a crescent or fan-shaped arrangement of either rough or delicately textured material. If you are planning colors that will blend with the lovely pink of the shell's interior, be sure that you don't conceal this with your flowers. The outside of many shells has a tan coat, which will dominate when the shell container is filled with your arrangement.

Manufacturers of novelty goods are producing interesting baskets, which are woven into unicorns and various other shapes that are fine for dried materials. Gift shops and florists' shops offer clever pottery containers and interesting novelties usually suitable for dried as well as fresh flowers. Antique shops are a source of such items as coffee mills and old scales, as well as lovely old glass and china pieces that make beautiful containers.

Photograph 45 shows two miniature arrangements both of which measure three inches or less. Needless to say, in making miniatures, a de-

44. The top of a bedpost placed on a hand-carved base which was once the lid of an old milk crock. It holds cockscomb, galax leaves, some of which have been rolled, and gracefully curved pods of the honey locust.

gree of dexterity is required, as well as a great deal of patience. You may find a pair of tweezers helpful in placing small plant material.

The containers for these in the photograph are, on the right, an acorn cup, and, on the left, a small inverted Oriental-poppy pod. You might use other pods or bottle caps as containers. The tops of the small wooden boxes that hold sewing-machine needles have a nice shape and the bare wood is good in color and texture. To prepare the containers for miniature arrangements, simply place a small ball of clay in the box tops or acorn cups. The pods will be cut off smoothly and the ball of clay placed on top. You will notice that the clay is on the cut end, the fluted crown of the pod down, forming the base of the container.

The acorn has a base, also, for without it, it would roll. In this case the base is the fluted crown of another poppy pod. It was cut with a sharp knife and glued to the botton of the acorn to form its base.

Dried-plant material for miniatures must be tiny, of course. As is true of all arranging, the size of the flower head should never exceed the diameter of the aperture of the container. In the acorn cup on the right of Photograph 45, three small blades of grass and three tiny nandina leaves make the outline. For the center of interest, very small strawflowers have been used.

The poppy pod holds tips of grasses, short bits of statice, xeranthemum, and the tiny terminal ends of larkspur. You might use any tiny flower or floret which you have accidentally broken in making a larger arrangement. Individual Chinese forget-me-nots and shreds of cockscomb are useful for miniatures.

Loving cups and mementoes of trips will find a place of greater importance in your home when filled with an array of colorful dried flowers.

For your boudoir dressing table, what could be more feminine than an old-fashioned jewelry box holding only beautifully dried roses and pressed rose leaves (see Photograph 46)?

These old jewel cases are frequently found in antique shops, their linings faded and torn. You will want to remove the lining from both the

45. These two miniature arrangements measure just three inches in height. On the left, the container is an Oriental poppy pod placed with its seed head down. The tiny bouquet is held by a ball of clay placed where the stem was cut. It is composed of larkspur, statice, xeranthemum, grasses, and pods. On the right, the cup of an acorn serves to hold three nandina leaves, three tiny strawflowers, and three grass tips.

box and its lid. The lid must be relined with satin, as it will form a background for the roses. In this jewel box a light shade of green was used. To hold the lining in place, use a heavy florist's wire bent in the shape of the box lid. This wire loop must be large enough to spring against the inside edges of the lid holding it in place. Cut the satin larger than the loop of wire, then fold the edges of the material over the wire. Place it in the lid of the box, the raw edges of the satin against the lid. The spring of the wire loop should be enough to hold the satin lining in position. Glue was not used, as it could so easily soil the lining. With your index finger, press against the satin in several places, giving it a soft tufted appearance.

The box itself need not be lined, as the dried flowers will hide its interior. Simply place a ball of clay close to the front of the box. Pressed rose leaves were added first, their backs toward the viewer. The under side of the rose leaves seemed to blend in color better with the green satin. Then came the dried rosebuds, and finally the opened roses.

If you are so unfortunate as to break a petal from a dried rose—or from many flowers—glue comes in very handy. Dip the broken end of the petal in glue and hold it for a few seconds to the spot where it separated from the flower.

46. An old-fashioned jewelry box becomes a beautiful setting for these perfectly preserved roses. The backs of the rose leaves blend with the green satin lining of the box. A ball of clay placed toward the front of the box holds the open roses, buds, and leaves.

VIII

Unusual Uses of Dried Material

Now that you have acquired the technique for designing charming arrangements for your coffee table, buffet, or desk, why not try something unusual? Here are some suggestions for making delightful compositions to hang on your wall, grace your banquet table, brighten your holidays, and even complete your costume! These may suggest others ways, completely original, of using your nicely dried blossoms.

Could anything be more charming for a boudoir than the hanging brush and mirror backs daintily decorated with nosegays of dried flowers shown in Photograph 47? These were a discarded dresser set made of plastic. The mirror was removed as well as the bristle part of the brush, leaving only the backs and handles. The inside of each has been painted a pale yellow. Balls of clay were pressed firmly along the inside edge of each back. Arrangements of strawflowers in pastel shades, yellow statice, pale-green hydrangea, blue larkspur, xeranthemum, all delicately edged with grasses, will stay pretty for months on your wall. Pale-green-satin ribbon bows, the same shade as the hydrangea, were tied to each handle to provide for hanging.

The antique frame supporting the colorful composition in Photograph 48 is handmade. The flowers pasted or wired to the green burlap back include yellow snapdragons, yellow statice, small dahlias, strawflowers, individual bells-of-Ireland, marigolds, cockscomb (which is old and has a somewhat yellowish cast), nigella pods, and nandina leaves. To make this effective "flower picture," cut cardboard to fit into the frame. Spread glue evenly over the entire surface of the cardboard. Stretch your material, in this case burlap, over the cardboard, smoothing it carefully from the center outward, and allow it to dry. Trim the material background even with the edge of the cardboard. Fasten it in your frame.

Now you are ready to start your flower design. Frequently the best results are had when you work out the design on paper. Or you can place your dried flowers on the background of the picture, arranging them in just

47. A discarded dresser set becomes a dainty wall hanging when decorated with delicately textured flowers and grasses. Find complete instructions for making in the text.

the pattern you want. However, the latter method necessitates more handling of the flowers and increases the chance of damage.

The design of a floral wall composition will depend on the décor of the room it is to grace and on your individual taste. The antique frame and floral picture in Photograph 48 would be suitable for a den or a room with wood-paneled walls. For a more formal room, you would want to use a more elegant frame, a background of velvet or a more delicate fabric, and daintier flowers such as larkspur, roses, and forget-me-nots.

Select plant material that is harmonious in texture and color with the frame and background. Then establish the outline. It may be roughly oval or it may follow the shape of the frame. Small leaves, either pressed or

48. This antique wooden frame displays a colorful picture of strawflowers, cockscomb, nigella pods, bells-of-Ireland, nandina foliage, statice, and snapdragons on a burlap background. It would be charming in a family room.

glycerinized, are appropriate in the outline, interspersed with small pods, sprays of little berries, statice, tips of grasses, or bits of goldenrod. These should all point out, the stems toward the center. Next will be a row of transitional material. Suitable for this are tiny chili peppers, pods, cockscomb, pearly everlasting, and pieces of hydrangea. The center will be the focal point, and will include the most dominant flowers: strawflowers, small zinnias, or perhaps pompon dahlias.

When you are thoroughly pleased with your design, start fastening each piece of dried-plant material to the background. This is done by gluing the smaller, lighter-weight pieces and wiring the heavier. The leaves will usually stay in place with a small amount of liquid all-purpose glue

49. Two orchids, sand-dried, are the center of interest in this shadow box. The floral picture is completed by the buds and blossoms of peonies, chrysanthemums, roses, gladioli, asters, and bits of hydrangea.

brushed on the back of each leaf. The leaf is then placed and held for a moment until the glue sets. Avoid too much glue, for it might spread out onto the material and be seen.

Pods, blossoms, or groups of florets that cannot be glued must be wired in place. This is done by bending a short length of wire into the shape of a hairpin or a staple and pushing the ends through the cardboard. Medium florist's wire is suitable for this. Then place the stem of the flower under the wire loop and bend the wire ends down on the back of the cardboard, stapling your flower securely to the cardboard. If the flower head is not completely stationary, a little glue under the head of the flower will remedy this. When you are through, you can flatten the wires that will be against the wall and, if you wish, paste heavy paper over the back for a neat appearance. This will also protect the wall.

Photograph 50 is another wall plaque, simple yet distinctive of line and texture. The design was made on a piece of wood which had been the back for an old picture. In our grandmothers' day, thin, roughly hewn lumber was used at the back of the frame to secure the picture in place. Its texture is rough and its color mellow.

A lotus pod, split in half, serves as the base for the floral design of okra pods and cane tops. To attach them to the board, the two halves of the lotus pod were first spread with glue, then held in place for several seconds. To secure them further, a thin shoe tack was hammered through the lower tip of each split pod into the wooden background. In the tops of all lotus pods are the distinguishing holes from which their seeds have dropped. These holes are convenient receptacles for the stems of the cane tops and okra pods, giving the appearance of a vase with its bouquet. The cane tops and okra pods are held in place by means of glue and shoe tacks.

In keeping with the rough-textured wooden background and plant material, a leather thong is used at the top of the plaque for the purpose of hanging it to the wall. Many of these plaques have been sold to profes-

50. A lotus pod, split in half, serves as the base for this floral design of okra pods and cane tops. The background is a thin, roughly hewn piece of lumber, once the back of an old picture. Note the leather-thong cord at the top in keeping with the texture of the plaque.

sional men for the waiting rooms of their offices. They are also charming in a paneled den or family room.

The frame of the plaque in Photograph 51 is a perfect foil with its rough texture and interesting bleached-gray color for the arrangement with driftwood. The frame was originally an ornate gilted antique found in a second-hand shop. The gilt and plaster-of-Paris beading were soaked from the frame by leaving wet cloths on it for several days. After it was scraped and allowed to dry, it acquired this handsome rough finish.

The background for the picture is burlap stretched over two thicknesses of heavy cardboard and tacked into the frame. Plywood could be used for this, but it is easier to push wire through the cardboard. Tiny inconspicuous holes were drilled in the driftwood and pods with an auger and wired to the background. Glycerinized magnolia leaves were secured by wire around the stem of each leaf. Several scales were removed from one side of the artichoke to allow it to fit more snugly against the burlap. Then it, too, was wired in place. Just below the driftwood is half a gourd mounted by means of a wire through two small holes drilled close to the edge.

A shadow box, such as is shown in Photograph 52, can be either hung or placed on a surface such as a buffet or desk. These come in many colors and can be bought at gift shops or at the florist's. The receding concave back, as well as the frame of this shadow box, has been painted Sheffield gray. A gold band outlines the face. Clay has been pressed along the lower inside surface to hold the arrangement. A portion of this clay was pulled

51. The frame of this plaque blends in color and texture with the bleached driftwood, dried artichoke and locust pods, and burlap background. The addition of the magnolia leaves (which have been glycerinized) and the half gourd completes the design.

52. This gold-rimmed shadow box decorated with dried flowers may either be hung on the wall or placed on a piece of furniture. Long-lasting larkspur, xeranthemum, strawflowers, lady's-thumb, and grasses are held in place by a roll of clay.

forward at the lower edge of the shadow box where those flowers were inserted which cover, or "break the line," of the container.

As with all designs, the line was established first, using tips of green feather grass and pink lady's-thumb. These curve, following the frame of the shadow box. Shorter tips of grass and lady's-thumb were placed to "break the line" of the container. Pink and orchid larkspur and white statice were used as a transition between the spike forms of the grasses and the round forms in the center of interest. Short pieces of larkspur were placed up into the clay around the lower edge of the shadow box. The center of interest was composed of pale-pink rosebuds, pink strawflowers, and orchid-colored xeranthemum.

A unique wall bracket, shown in Photograph 53, has been made from an old-fashioned tin brush and comb holder. This relic was once familiar in farm homes in bygone days when Father and the hired men came to the house for dinner. It hung above the washstand on an outside wall in the summertime holding a comb and brush. The little square mirror allowed the men to admire themselves while "cleaning up" for dinner. In the winter the comb and brush holder was brought inside.

In preparing this antique for use, the entire brush and comb holder was painted a dull black. A ball of clay in each pocket of the bracket supports branches of brightly colored bittersweet.

The silver candelabrum shown in Photograph 54 is lovely for a formal dinner table or in pairs on a buffet. Its individual epergnette holds a candle encircled with a nosegay of fine-textured dried flowers. Usually the epergnette—that is, the removable bowl that holds the candle and flowers—is made of glass.

To make the dried arrangement, take the glass epergnette out of the candelabrum and rest it on a tea cup, as it will not stand erect by itself. Remove the candle, but allow space for it while preparing the design. Soften a ball of clay—if possible, green clay—and roll it between your

53. This old-fashioned tin brush and comb holder once hung above the washstand in an old farmhouse. Decorated with the bright orange and gold berries of the bittersweet, it would grace any home.

54. What could be more useful to the busy homemaker than this candelabrum holding a dainty bouquet always ready to enhance the most elaborate dinner table or buffet? This epergnette is decorated with larkspur, roses, hydrangea, xeranthemum, statice, strawflowers, and grasses.

hands until it becomes ropelike and is about an inch in diameter. Place this around the base of the candle holder in the epergnette, firming it with your finger tips.

The color and texture of the flowers used in the design will be dictated by the table setting. Keep in mind the colors in the china, the table linen to be used, and the room itself.

The principle of design follows closely that of the bouquet made in the rice bowl described in Chapter VII. Looking down on the epergnette, space larkspur or tips of grass around the center, not in an exact circle, but staggered artistically. View your design from all sides to be sure that it has balance and symmetry. Next add material such as statice or feathery tips of cockscomb to curve gracefully over the edge of the epergnette, spacing them irregularly. Fill in with dainty flowers such as small roses and rosebuds, daisies, xeranthemum, acroclinium, forget-me-nots, or bits of hydrangea. Space and distribute your colors so that the arrangement will present somewhat the same appearance from all sides. Remember that spike shapes will give it depth.

Costume jewelry can be made from the more hardy flowers you have dried, such as strawflowers, xeranthemum, or achillea. Lapel pins decorated with dried flowers and matching earrings would make unusual gifts. And for yourself, design several sets to match your costumes. If they do not last too long, the flowers can easily be replaced with very little or no expense.

Earrings can best be made by using strawflowers that are extremely sturdy and come in a variety of colors and sizes. Use the earring bases sold at most ten-cent stores. For each earring, trim the stem close to the head of a strawflower and dab it with all-purpose liquid glue. Hold it firmly against the earring base until the glue sets and allow it to dry.

ARRANGEMENTS FOR SPECIAL OCCASIONS

Holidays are gayer when the home reflects the spirit of these merry occasions. You can provide some very unusual holiday decorations for Christmas, Thanksgiving, and Valentine's Day by planning ahead to have the necessary dried material.

For Christmas, try spraying your entire arrangement silver or gold. Pressurized cans of gilt or aluminum paint, which can be purchased at most hardware stores, make the work of painting your dried materials much easier and prettier than brushed-on paint. Make an arrangement on a board or an old platter using only a ball of clay to hold your materials. As it will be painted, you need not be concerned with the color of the dried plants. Study only the shapes and outlines for interesting combinations. Leaves, grains, and pods, rather than blossoms, are more appropriate for spraying. Try establishing the design with gracefully curved shafts of

wheat, filling in with sea oats, and milkweed pods, and using dried magnolia leaves at the base of the arrangement. Then, after you are satisfied
with the outline and design, spray both container and arrangement either
gold or silver.

A group of Christmas balls wired together make a dramatic focal point
for the all-gold or all-silver arrangement. Or buy a few fresh red carnations
at the florist's for the center of interest in a silver or all-white arrangement.
Water in a small glass tube will keep the flowers fresh.

While the paint is wet, try sprinkling Christmas glitter (available at
the ten-cent stores during Christmas) on the leaves: it is very effective.

If you prefer to protect your container from the paint, you can mask
it with tape or one of the plastic coverings, and then remove it when the
arrangement is dry.

55. For Christmas, spray an entire arrangement of magnolia
leaves, small pine cones, and gracefully curved twigs with a
dull white paint. When it is dry place three colored Christmas balls as the center of interest.

56. Beautiful floral compositions on the altar enhance any religious service. The magnolia leaves, gladiolus foliage, sea oats, and artificial grapes were all sprayed a full white. While the paint was still wet, powdered bronze was blown along the central vein of the leaves and was used to highlight the grapes. Apples (these were fresh, but artificial could be used) were dipped in the paint and then burnished with bronze. Florist's picks and clay secure the arrangements in the containers.

Gracefully curved roots and branches sprayed white are lovely to use with fresh evergreens at Christmas. For such an arrangement, you might use as a container a wood base or a board painted white. Place a mound of clay slightly off center and arrange the white roots or branches in an artistic design. A figurine of the Madonna would make a lovely center of interest placed before the clay. Between the white branches and the figure, you could use fresh evergreens such as blue spruce. White magnolia leaves are also lovely in this setting. Groups of processed galax leaves brushed lightly with gold or silver paint (but with their centers still showing green) might be more suitable, depending on the coloring of the figurine. Instead of galax leaves, trimmings from any shrub whose leaves will dry naturally on the stem, such as boxwood, could be lightly sprayed with gold or silver to complete your composition.

The figure of a deer could be used instead of the Madonna. Also, at Christmas the stores offer little candles in the shape of angels, choirboys, and snowmen, which make gay centers of interest.

57. For Thanksgiving, a colorful composition can be made on a flat wooden
board. These two ceramic pheasants gaze into a colorful collection of strawflowers, achillea, and dock, wondering, perhaps, if that calico corn is edible. At
the base are small gourds, flanked by brilliantly colored lichens found in the
woods. Miniature cattails and bearded wheat complete the picture.

If you prefer to use plant materials for your focal point, paint the inside of several milkweed pods a bright red. Wire these together to form the petals of a poinsettia. You will need to attach artificial wire stems to each pod first. The center of the simulated flower might be three tiny gold Christmas balls each on a wire grouped with the red milkweed petals.

Another unusual "focal point" would be a cluster of grapes made of nuts (see Figure 8). Hazel nuts can be used, or any small, round nut. Drive a tack almost all the way into the end of a nut, leaving enough space for a wire to be wrapped just under the tack head for a stem. Copper wire is very pretty for the stems, as some of them may be seen. Gather these copper stems together for a graceful grouping of your artificial grapes. The tiny green tendrils that are associated with grapes can be made of the copper wire; wrap the wire around a pencil, making about eight to ten turns. Slip out the pencil and attach the wire at one end to the top of the grape cluster. Pull the tendril of copper wire gently to give it a natural look.

Thanksgiving and fall bring thoughts of harvest, when gourds and squash are ripe and the colorful ears of corn are ready to be gathered. In Photograph 57, two ceramic pheasants are reminders that it is hunting season, too. The arrangement was made on an oval walnut-stained board that held only a ball of clay. The design was outlined with miniature cattails and bearded wheat. Then came colorful ears of calico corn, achillea, and strawflowers. Tiny gourds and lichens were placed at the base. The two pheasants, whose colors blend with those of the dried-plant material, complete the picture.

Frequently dried materials will give a thin appearance and need to be backed by some foliage, even though it may not be clearly visible. Pressed

Figure 8. This unusual "cluster of grapes" is really a group of nuts wired together to form the cluster. Copper wire, first wound on a pencil, is used to make the tendrils.

autumn leaves back this arrangement to give it a more substantial look, especially if it is to be placed against a light background.

When you are using heavy ears of corn, or vegetables or fruits, it is necessary to find a means of supporting them and holding them in position. Usually impaling them on the sharp ends of florists' picks and thrusting the other end into a ball of clay will be sufficient. However, if these are not long enough for the required height in your design, you can sharpen sturdy sticks for the fruit or vegetables, then place them in the clay.

For Valentine's Day, what could be more expressive of the sweetest of all sentiments than the old-fashioned valentine in Photograph 58? This would be charming as a centerpiece for a buffet table.

The base is plywood, spread with glue and covered with blue velvet. The material was pulled tightly over the edges of the wooden base and secured with glue. A ball of clay is needed to hold the floral design. If it is difficult to make the clay adhere to the velvet, as it was in this case, cut a hole in the cloth and place the clay directly against the wood.

A pattern for the heart was first drawn on paper, then cut from cardboard and covered with the same shade of blue velvet. To strengthen it, a wire coat hanger was bent into the same size and shape of the heart, the two ends of the wire jutting an inch or so from the base of the heart. The extended wire ends become necessary when placing it in the ball of clay. The wire was then fastened to the back of the heart. To finish the heart, the edge of a paper doily was ruffled and sewn to the velvet, allowing about an inch to show from the front. Place the heart, thrusting the ends of the wire into the ball of clay.

An old-fashioned bouquet of pastel-colored xeranthemum, statice, bits of hydrangea, and cockscomb with larkspur and strawflowers conceals the ball of clay. Notice that the lines of the floral design unify the heart with its velvet-covered base.

58. For Valentine's Day, what could be sweeter than an old-fashioned velvet heart, complete with dainty lace trimming? At its base is an arrangement of pink, white, and blue larkspur, bits of hydrangea and cockscomb with straw-flowers and xeranthemum. Directions for making the heart, the plywood base, and the floral design are given in the text.

IX

Caring for Dried Arrangements

While it is true that dried flowers require a minimum of attention, some care must be exercised in order that they stay colorful and in good condition for as long a period as possible. How disappointing to process plants and create a beautiful design only to have them fade and droop for want of care.

The place where a dried arrangement is displayed should be free from drafts and not in direct sunlight. Usually, processed-plant material is used more in the winter than in the summer. This is all to the good, as the house is drier where there is furnace heat. Dried flowers need to be kept dry to stay pretty. Avoid all dampness.

Keeping your arrangement free from dust is not a problem if you use a feather for this process. Its flexible tip will reach into and around the daintiest florets and delicate spikes. A camel's-hair brush is good for larger, more rugged material and for foliage. Glycerinized leaves can be wiped clean with a damp cloth.

You will find that some of the dried material in your arrangement will last longer than others. You may want to freshen the whole composition occasionally by replacing a few pieces that have begun to droop. Or you may tire of the whole design after a while and decide to remake it, saving the best material to use later.

To take your arrangement apart, start from the back, removing the outer stems first, being careful not to damage the brittle material. It is well to work on newspaper, sorting the material as you remove it, each kind to itself. This will help you when you start on your new design.

If you have used clay, clean any shattered material from it and work it into a ball. Wrap it in wax paper or aluminum foil. Clean your container well before putting it away. Why not try a different container, using a different design? Add a new center of interest, perhaps, to the dried material that has remained in good condition, and you will be delighted at the result. Or you may want to store the material in boxes to be used at a later date.

HOW TO TRANSPORT ARRANGEMENTS
BOTH FRESH AND DRIED

The problem of transporting either a fresh or dried arrangement without disarranging it is one that has often baffled flower lovers. If you are planning to take your floral composition to a flower show or an exhibit, it usually has to be remade by the time it has undergone the rigors of being handled while riding in a car. However, using the following methods when you are responsible for altar flowers in your church, you can make the arrangement ahead of time and take it to the sanctuary in the certainty that it will look the same on the altar as it did on your kitchen table. Your friends in the hospital will be pleased with arrangements that you have made with care and artistry at home and brought to them in perfect condition.

Dried arrangements, properly placed in boxes by the following methods, may be transported any distance. Indeed, they have been taken by car across the United States and arrived still in good condition. They could be transported by train or plane in boxes if carried by the arranger. That is, they are not to be shipped by the usual methods, as the boxes must be carefully handled by one who appreciates their delicate contents.

If you are transporting as many as four arrangements, select a large, strong cardboard carton whose height is about the height of the tallest arrangement, and whose breadth is more than the width of the largest arrangement. If you are planning to take your compositions only a few miles within the city, you may cut the top of the box completely away. Also, a tall arrangement may exceed the height of the box by a few inches without damage, as you will carry it carefully, seeing that the top does not contact a car door or any other obstacle.

If you are planning a longer trip by auto, train, or plane, leave the top of the box joined to one side of the carton and push it back out of the way. Later it can be lowered over its load and taped or tied with twine in place. In the latter case, of course, the height of the box must exceed the tallest arrangement.

With a sharp knife, cut down two adjacent corners of the carton from the top to the bottom, or floor, of the box (see Photograph 59). This will allow you to open the front panel, so to speak, bending it flat to the floor, and will permit room for you to work inside. Use the larger width of the box for this purpose. This panel will later be taped back into place.

Now set the arrangements that are made to be viewed from one side only against the wall of the box. Three of such designs can be placed in a large box with their flat sides to the walls. A fourth arrangement may fit in the center, anchored to the floor of the carton with clay. This arrangement could be made "in the round" to be viewed from all sides, as it will not touch the box. See that there is ample room between arrangements

59. To transport arrangements, select a strong cardboard carton large enough to accommodate your flowers. By cutting slits in the sides of the box, you may tie your arrangements securely in place with strips of cloth. See text for complete instructions.

so that none touches; neither should they contact the corners of the box. In this first step, you are planning how to place each arrangement so that it will fit in with the others.

Next, remove all but one arrangement placed against the back wall of the box. With a pencil draw a line on the carton on each side of the container at its widest point, starting about an inch below the top of the container to an inch from the floor of the box. Remove the arrangement and cut two parallel slits along these lines through which you will thread strips of cloth to tie the container securely in place.

60. For arrangements which are "in the round," as in this rice bowl or in other low containers, anchor to the floor of the box with softened clay.

The strips of cloth—old pieces of sheeting would do nicely—should be torn about five to six inches in width, depending on the height of your container, and long enough to pull through the slits and tie.

Pull one end of the cloth from the inside through to the outside of the box. Then put the other end into the other slit on the inside of the box and pull it through also, each pulled only a few inches, leaving a loop of cloth inside the box. Replace the arrangement inside this loop and pull the cloth up and around the container. Now pull on each end equally so as not to turn the container as it rests on the box, and tie the ends of the cloth together on the outside. Make the knot secure yet one that can be easily untied.

The other arrangements are placed in the box in the same way. You will probably have room for a fourth arrangement, either a round one or a flat one as it will not touch the box. This can be placed in the center and anchored with clay.

This second method of securing the container to the box by means of clay is best for transporting any arrangement that cannot be tied with strips of cloth, such as miniatures, those made in shallow or flat containers, and those made in the round, to be viewed from all sides. Place such an arrangement in the box so that it does not touch the sides of the box or any other arrangement. Soften several balls of clay between your hands. Then mash each firmly against the base of the container and the floor of the box, molding the two together. Add more until you have made a clay collar completely around the foot of the arrangement.

If you are transporting only one arrangement, of course, you will need a box only large enough to hold it without touching the sides. If you are carrying fresh flowers, be sure to remove most of the water, leaving only enough to keep the cut ends of the flowers wet. If you are not going far and your flowers are well conditioned, you may remove all the water.

After the last arrangement is secured to the box either by clay or by strips of cloth, bend the open front panel back into place and tape it securely. If you are traveling a distance, replace the lid of the box and tape it securely.

With reasonable care exercised during the trip—that is, seeing that the box is always held upright and sustains no jolts—your arrangements should be in perfect condition when you arrive at your destination.

ENJOYING THE FRUITS OF YOUR LABORS

There is no end of the use you can make of your dried-plant materials. It is hoped that these pages will suggest ideas and means for making your surroundings more enjoyable. Don't overlook your husband's office or reception room as a spot for a lasting bouquet or the wall of his den for a plaque made of preserved woods' materials.

Gifts of dried arrangements are always welcome, especially for the hospital patient, whose fresh flowers often wither in a day or two. Gifts for Christmas or any special occasion will be long-remembered reminders of your affection if they are dried and arranged by the giver.

Index

Absorption, of flower's moisture, 24
Achillea, 98, 111; best variety, 49; cutting, 49; drying, 49
Acorn cup, as container, 100; Photo. 45
Acroclinium, 92
Ageratum, hung to dry, 37; sand-dried, 37
Air-drying, a method of preserving, 64; forsythia foliage, 64; buddleia, 64; gladiolus, 64; magnolia foliage, 64; nandina, 64
Alba poplar leaves, glycerinized, 71
Altar arrangement, 11, Photo. 56
Alum, for flower drying, 18
Apple blossoms, sand-dried, 39
Area for drying, 16
Area for hanging plants, 42
Arranging, principles of, for good design, 76 ff.
Asters, dried like roses, 30
Artemisia, 82, 91
    best variety, 51; cutting, 51; drying, 51; drying period, 51
Artichoke, and driftwood, 108, Photo. 51, used in design, 108
Artificial flowers, 13
Artificial foliage, 13
Attic for drying flowers, 16
Autumn leaves, pressed, 116, 117

Bachelor's buttons, sand-dried, 38
Balance in flower arranging, 77
Bearded wheat, 13, 116
Bedpost container, 98, Photo. 44
Beech 90, Photo. 37
Beech foliage, glycerinized, 67
Beech leaves, pressed, 66
Beechdrops, 56; how to dry, 56
Bells of Ireland, 103; using wire in stem, 32; sand-dried; 32; how to obtain curve with, 32
Berries, 77
Berries, nandina, 55; bramble, 55; bittersweet, 55; pyracantha, 55
Black-eyed Susan, sand-dried, 37, 13

Borax for drying flowers, 18
Bottles, small-mouthed for glycerine solution, 20
Box, for holding sand, 24
Box, for transporting arrangements, 120, 121, 122, Photo. 59, 60
Boxes for storing dried material, 16
Boxwood, sprayed, 114
Branches and twigs in arranging, 93
Branches, bare, good for "line," 57; treatment and use, 57
"Breaking the line of the container," rule for, 78, 87
Bridal wreath, cutting, 22, 49; drying, 49; drying period, 49
Brittleness of dried flowers, 15
Brush and comb holder, as container, 110, Photo. 53
Brush and mirror back, used as container, 103, Photo. 47
Buddleia, sand-dried, 31
Buddleia leaves, air-dried, 64
Burs, used in arranging, 55; castor bean, 55; chestnut, 55; chinguapin, 55; drying period, 55
Butterfly bush foliage, pressed, 65

Calyx of a rose, 25
Calyxes, in arrangements, drying, 51; gladiolus calyx, 51; rose of Sharon calyx, 51; poplar calyx, 51
Cane top, 107
Care of dried arrangements, 15, 119 ff.; re-making a design, 119, 120
Carnations, sand-dried, 24, 29
Cartons, cardboard, for holding sand, 17, 18
Cattails, harvesting, 22, 60, 115; drying, 60; miniature, 60
Cattail foliage, 22
Celosia. See Cockscomb
Chili peppers, 105
Chestnut bur, 55
Chestnuts, Photo. 38

COMPLETE LIST OF
PLANT MATERIALS FOR DRYING

This is an alphabetical list of almost all plant material suitable for drying. Some plants dry better in sand, some by hanging, etc. The best method for each is indicated by a symbol in this chart.

H denotes drying by hanging. **S** denotes drying in sand. **S** followed by *R* means sand-drying similar to **Roses**. **S** followed by *L* means sand-drying similar to **Larkspur**. **S** followed by *Z* means sand-drying similar to **Zinnias**. **G** denotes processing with solution of glycerine. **P** denotes pressing. These drying methods are thoroughly described in the book.

Achillea See Yarrow	H	**Crabgrass** *(Panicum)*	H
Acroclinium *(Helipterum roseum)*	H	**Dahlia** *(Dahlia)*	S R
Ageratum *(Ageratum)*	H	**Daisy**	
Alba Poplar *(Populus alba)*	G	*(Chrysanthemum leucanthemum)*	S Z
Apple Blossom *(Malus)*	S	**Delphinium** *(Delphinium cultorum)*	S L
Aster *(Aster)*	S Z	**Dock** *(Rumex obtusifolius)*	H
Autumn Leaves	P	**Dogwood** *(Cornus florida)*	S Z
		Dogwood Leaves *(Cornus florida)*	G
Bachelor's-Button			
(Centaurea Cyanus)	S Z	**Feather** or **Velvet Grass**	
Bayberries *(Myrica)*	H	*(Holcus lanatus)*	H
Beech Drops *(Epifagus virginiana)*	H	**Fern, Christmas**	
Beech Foliage *(Fagus)*	P or G	*(Polystichum acrostichoides)*	P
Bells of Ireland *(Molucella laevis)*	S L	**Ficus decor** *(Ficus decor)*	H
Bittersweet *(Celastrus)*	H	**Forsythia** *(Forsythia)*	S L
Black-eyed Susan *(Rudbeckia hirta)*	S Z	**Forsythia Leaves** *(Forsythia)*	P or G
Bluegrass *(Poa pratensis)*	H	**Foxtail Grass** *(Setaria glauca)*	H
Bramble or **Greenbrier Berries**			
(Smilax)	H	**Galax Leaves** *(Galax aphylla)*	P or G
Bridal Wreath *(Spiraea prunifolia)*	H	**Gladiolus** *(Gladiolus)*	S L
Buckeye *(Aesculus octandra)*	H	**Gladiolus, Calyx** *(Gladiolus)*	H
Butter-and-Eggs *(Linaria vulgaris)*	S L	**Globe-Amaranth**	
Butterfly Bush Foliage *(Buddleia)*	P	*(Gomphrena globosa)*	H
		Goldenrod *(Solidago)*	H
Calendula *(Calendula officinalis)*	S Z	**Gourds** *(Cucurbita)*	H
Carnation *(Dianthus)*	S R	**Ground Cherries** *(Physalis)*	H
Castor-Bean Leaves *(Ricinus)*	G		
Catalpa Pods *(Catalpa)*	H	**Hazelnut** *(Corylus americana)*	H
Chestnut Foliage		**Helipterum**	
(Castanea dentata)	P or G	*(Helipterum Humboldtianum)*	H
Chinese Forget-Me-Not		**Henbane** *(Hyoscyamus niger)*	H
(Cynoglossum amabile)	S L	**Hickory Nut** *(Carya)*	H
Chinese Lantern *(Physalis Alkekengi)*	H	**Hollyhock** *(Althaea)*	S L
Chinquapin *(Castanea pumila)*	H	**Honesty** or **Money Plant** *(Lunaria)*	H
Chrysanthemum *(Chrysanthemum)*	S Z	**Honey Locust Pods** *(Gleditsia)*	H
Cockscomb *(Celosia)*	H	**Hydrangea, "Hills-of-Snow"**	
Corn, Calico or **Rainbow** *(Zea Mays)*	H	*(Hydrangea)*	H
Corn, Indian *(Zea Mays)*	H	**Hydrangea** *(Hydrangea paniculate)*	H